LINK UP

By the same author

What's your opinion?
Things that matter

LINK UP

Selected by
Philip Grosset

Evans Brothers Limited, London

Published by Evans Brothers Limited
Montague House, Russell Square, London, WC1B 5BX

First published 1971
Reprinted 1974, 1976, 1978

ISBN 0 237 28485 5   PRA 5789
Filmset by Photoprint Plates Limited, Rayleigh, Essex
Printed by William Clowes & Sons, Limited
London, Beccles and Colchester

Contents

Acknowledgements

Introduction 9

Human Embryo Development 11

Growth and Development 12

Togetherness 17

Behaving like Apes? 19

Evolution? 22

We're Grown-up! 24

At School 25

Summerhill School 26

Girls' Magazines—Then and Now 32

Young People—At the Turn of the Century and Now 34

Agonies of Adolescence 36

Schoolgirls see the future boss as 'Prince Charming' 37

Away from Home 38

London 40

On the Way to Work 41

First Day at Work 42

Happy at Work? 43

Factory Time 48

Workman's Hand 50

The Clerk 51

People at Work 53

Young Workers Get Too Much Money 56

Stimulating the Animal Emotions 57

Valuable 60

Who Am I? 62

The Swedish Answer: Unisex Marriage 65

Home Sweet Home 66

The Good Old Days 68

How Things Used to Be 70

Your Country Expects . . . 72

Why Patriots Are a Bit Nuts in the Head 73

Guernica 73

All Done in Sport 74

Absurd Animal 76

Factory Farming 77

The Advance of Science 78

Just Around the Corner 80

No Morning After 84

First Men on the Moon 86

You'll Make a Million Bucks Up There! 87

The Andromeda Nebula 96

Space Travel 97

Starscope 98

Horoscopes 99

The Witch Doctor 101

Your Sunday Paper 102

Nuts to the Neophiliacs! 104

How I Became a Prostitute 105

A Tax on Babies 106

Now Marcella is Having the Last Laugh 107

5 Ways to Kill a Man 108

Sometime During Eternity 110

Brides of Christ 112

God? 115

Meeting Human Needs 116

New Approach Needed 117

Come Down Lord From Your
Heaven 118

Try Some Purple Hearts and You'll
See a Whole New Way of Life 119

We are Happy but Most of the
World is Hungry 120

The Young and the Old 122

Resurrection 124

Invitation 126

Acknowledgements

For permission to quote from copyright material in this book, the author and publishers are indebted to: Consumers' Association for the article 'Horoscopes' from *Which* June 1969; *The Daily Telegraph* for the article 'Schoolgirls see the future boss as "Prince Charming"' by John Izbicki; *The Daily Telegraph* and Mrs Sara Jolly for her article 'The Swedish Answer: Unisex Marriage'; Darton, Longman & Todd Limited for the extract from *We Are Happy* edited by Ralph Ricketts; André Deutsch Limited for 'Absurd Animal' from *Dust Falls on Eugene Schlumberger* by Shena Mackay; Victor Gollancz Limited for an extract from *Profiles of the Future* by Arthur C. Clarke, and for an extract from *Summerhill* by A. S. Neill; William Heinemann Medical Books Limited for an extract from *Adolescence* by T. A. A. Hunter and M. E. M. Hereford; David Higham Associates Limited for 'No Morning After' from *Tales of Ten Worlds* by Arthur C. Clarke; Hope Leresche & Steele for the poem 'Why Patriots are a Bit Nuts in the Head' by Roger McGough, taken from *Penguin Modern Poets 10*, published by Penguin Books Limited; Arthur James Limited for an extract from *The Forgotten People* by Norman S. Power; Longman Group Limited for the poem 'Valuable' from *The Frog Prince* by Stevie Smith; Lorna Music Company Limited for the song 'Come Down Lord From Your Heaven' by Judith Piepe and Stephen Delft; MacGibbon & Kee for the poems 'London' and 'Sometime during Eternity' from *An Eye on the World* by Lawrence Ferlinghetti; *New Statesman* for the poem 'New Approach Needed' by Kingsley Amis; *News of the World* for the article 'A Tax on Babies'; *The Observer Foreign News Service* for the article 'Agonies of Adolescence' by Christine Doyle; Penguin Books Limited for the extracts from 'Factory Time' by Dennis Johnson and 'The Clerk' by Philip Callow, both taken from *Work* edited by Ronald Fraser, and for the extracts from *The Family and Marriage in Britain* by Ronald Fletcher and *Psychology for Everyman* by Larry S. Skurnik and Frank George, and for the poems '5 Ways to Kill a Man' by Edwin Brock (taken from *Penguin Modern Poets 8*) and 'Resurrection' by Vladimir Holan, translated by George Theiner (taken from *New Writing in Czechoslovakia*); *The People* for the articles 'How I became a prostitute' and 'Nuts to the Neophiliacs!'; Routledge & Kegan Paul Limited for extracts from *Adolescent Boys of East London* by Peter Willmott; Professor Roy Shaw and ABC Television Limited for the article from *Your Sunday Paper* edited by Richard Hoggart; *The Sunday Times Magazine* for the article 'Brides of Christ' by Pauline Peters; Thames and Hudson Limited for an extract from *The Biological Time Bomb* by G. Rattray Taylor, and for an extract from *The Evolution of Man* by David Pilbeam.

Every attempt has been made to contact all copyright holders concerning material in this book.

Illustrations

(Note: Where two illustrations appear on a page, t refers to the top and b to the bottom of the page.)

Introduction

The contents of this book are arranged in rough chronological order following man's life from before birth to after death. So, if you begin at the beginning, you will often find there is a more or less natural progression in which each item links up with the next.

However, there is no reason why you should not start on any page you like. Suppose your interest is caught by the contrast between the girls' magazines on pages 32 and 33. This might start you wondering in what other ways our society has changed since 1884 (see pages 15, 18, 34, 35, 37–38, 40, 43–46, 53, 54, 56–65, 68–71, 77–79, 102–107, 118, 119, 122 and the front and back covers). Or you might like to discuss teenage comics (see pages 62–64, 87–95 and 98). Or you might wonder about the advantages, or otherwise, of living in a 'permissive' society (see pages 18, 23, 26–31, 35, 56–61, 102–105, 107, 118, 119 and 122) or query the position of women in the modern world (see pages 35, 40, 53, 57, 59–66, 68–72, 94, 105, 107, 112–114, 116, and 122).

Once you begin to link up items in this way, you will find that all sorts of contrasts and comparisons begin to emerge. There are no lists of questions for it is hoped that every reader will want to ask his own. Look, for example, at the photographs on the front and back covers. What do they suggest to you? The picture on the front cover starts me thinking about race relations, prejudice, childhood influences, environment, education, love, sex and having children. The picture on the back cover makes me think of spoiling the countryside, pollution, planned obsolescence, and traffic problems. Link up the pictures and I, at least, begin to wonder whether human beings are more than decaying machines, and to consider the dangers of ever-increasing waste, over-population, the quality of life and what God intends of it all—if He exists at all.

You can find more about most of these subjects and about many others—not all of them so serious—in this book, which will, I hope, prove a stimulating starting point for further discovery and discussion.

PHILIP GROSSET

Human Embryo Development

At 24 days the head (top) and tail regions are distinguishable. Two days later the gill arches are visible to the right of the head, and the umbilical cord has become a definite entity. After four weeks the limbs have appeared, and by eight weeks the digits are outlined. Also by this time the tail has disappeared, and the face has started to develop. By nine weeks the neck is recognizable, the spine has straightened so that the head becomes erect, and the external features of the eye, nose and ear have appeared.

4 days

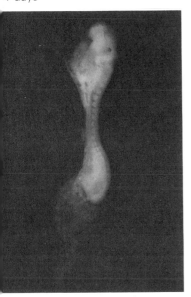

26 days

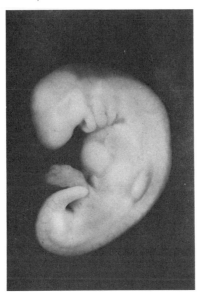

4 weeks

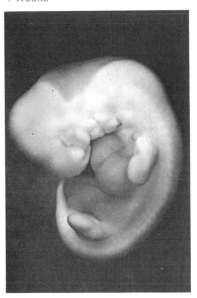

$5\frac{1}{2}$ weeks

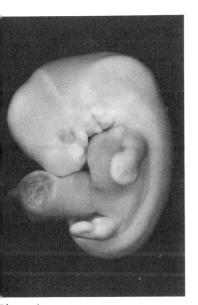

8 weeks

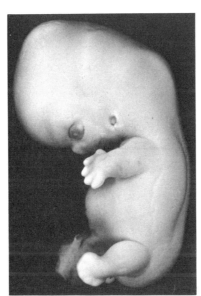

9 weeks

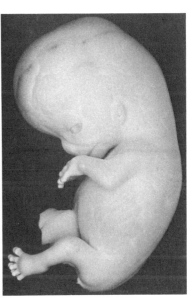

Growth and Development

The two main influences which affect our development are inherited potential and environmental experience. Our inborn characteristics determine our constitution as members of the human species: they determine skin colour, eye colour, bone structure, and internal make-up. These inborn traits govern in a real sense the rate of growth and the limits of biological and physical development. The second influence, that of learning and experience, nurtures this potential so that normal, healthy growth progresses to maturity. We reach adulthood through the cumulative and combined effects of these two influences.

From the moment of birth, the child appears as a feeding, crying, sleeping, body-waste producer, not very different from any other infant creature.

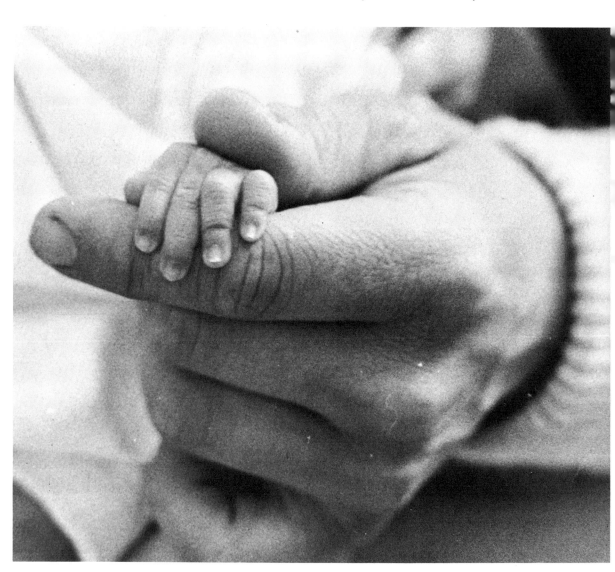

None of the human characteristics, such as speech, thought, sociability, and so on, are apparent. Within a few weeks the child's muscles mature enough for him to be able to focus his eyes on things and people around him, and show an awareness of his environment. The reflex patterns of behaviour that are inborn include sucking, breathing, and the other body functions. The infant is so helpless that he cannot even perform such basic survival responses as escape from pain-causing stimuli, or obtaining food and drink, without adult assistance. By six months he can sit up, and at the end of the first year he is usually able to stand or crawl around. Within two or three months more he is on his feet and walking without assistance. Speech development takes place in a somewhat similar manner. In the early months the only sounds are crying or babbling noises. After six months, distinct learned speech sounds can be made, such as 'mamama' and 'dadada'. By the first year these have become 'Mama' and 'Daddy', and are associated with particular people. Although the spoken vocabulary is quite limited at this age, quite a few commands and demands can be clearly understood by the child, such as 'sit still' or 'open wide', or 'don't touch that'. By about fifteen months the child is able to issue one-word demands or comments such as 'out' or 'doll'. Soon, the words are connected in crude but meaningful combinations of two or three words: 'me want sweet' and 'me play toys'. The child is now becoming a human being, to be influenced by the experiences which make people social. Research with animals and humans has shown, however, that our psychological needs and motives may be significantly influenced from the day of birth, if not before. The importance of the sense of touch and other forms of early behaviour experience has been highlighted by studies of monkeys brought up in isolation with only a choice of substitute mothers to comfort them. One of the 'mothers' was a roughly monkey-shaped construction of wire, with an indentation

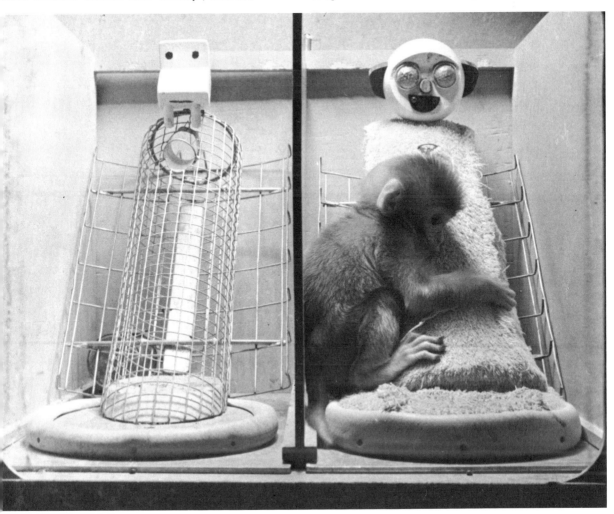

in its 'chest' where a milk-filled bottle could be sucked so that nourishment could be obtained in the normal way. The other 'mother' was a frame of wire, covered in sponge and wrapped in towelling material. This one was for some of the animals also provided with a source of nourishment. Nearly all the monkeys, regardless of which 'mother' had the bottle, spent virtually all of their time in the presence of the soft, cuddly substitute mother. Not only was she a comfortable thing to cling to but, when the young animals were frightened, they returned to her as the source of protection and safety. The experience and association with the cuddly substitute mother was long-lasting, and when a monkey was returned to her after a full year of separation he demonstrated a very real affection and pleasure at the reunion.

These experiments, reported by Dr Harry Harlow of Wisconsin University, were originally intended to test the relative strengths of the oral and sucking need against the need for contact-comfort. The studies demonstrated the greater importance of the sense of touch in these animals, but they also brought out some very startling side effects.

When the monkeys, brought up in isolation, were put in cages with others of the opposite sex, with the intention of breeding from them, it was found that they were all very antisocial! Not only would they not associate with each other, but those few who tried to engage in the sex act were just not able to assume a correct posture. Most of the monkeys were without any sex drive, instinct or the 'savoir faire' necessary for reproduction! This was most disturbing. If the monkeys would not breed, an enormous cost would have to be borne to continue the experiments.

Dr Harlow set a couple of normal male monkeys to engage some of the reluctant females in sexual activities. As a result of the skill and patience of these 'Romeos' some of the females became pregnant. When they gave birth to their offspring, however, they treated them as unwanted children, or abandoned them altogether. These females appeared to be without maternal drive or mothering instincts.

Although, of course, it would be wrong to draw firm conclusions about human behaviour on the basis of these studies of monkeys, Dr Harlow's experiments strongly suggest that contact-comfort may be very important to a child. They also suggest that isolation during very early childhood can lead to: (a) antisocial behaviour as an adult, (b) absence of interest or ability to engage in sexual affairs, and (c) among the females, a lack of maternal drive. These

motivational consequences were completely unexpected and are now being intensively studied in an effort to throw more light upon types of childhood experiences and their relationship with motivation in later life. Orphanages, where similar results of behaviour disturbance were once observed, today try to make provision for every child to receive, as a protective measure, a daily 'dose' of love and affection from some adult.

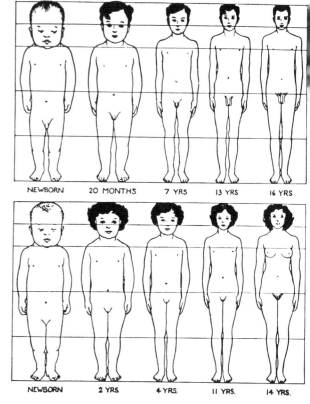

The first five years of human life, spent mostly at home, are characterized by development of language, motor ability, and socialization. The child, however, is quite self-centred in his view of life and generally does not know how to cooperate with other children in play or other activities. Children at this age may play in the same location but there is no genuine understanding one for the other. School experiences, however, open up a whole new world for the child. He learns to become partly independent of his mother and his home. He learns new facts of life, such as the distinction between the sexes, emphasized by the different toilet arrangements. He learns to conform to a greater extent than might have been the case at home. School uniforms, communal meals, scheduled play and rest periods, all are part of the

EARLY YEARS

Bradford schoolchildren in 1900

Bradford schoolchildren today

school experiences of learning how to behave in society.

As the child matures he develops more complex powers of reasoning. With exposure to stimulating material in the school environment the child rapidly acquires many intellectual skills, including the ability to use symbols such as letters and numbers. This acquisition of knowledge is also integrated with the development of other skills, such as the ability to play certain games, the use of artistic materials, tools, etc., and the formation of attitudes. The schools are charged with the task of inculcating knowledge and also moulding the children into useful members of their community and society. To achieve these multiple objectives the schools include recreational activities as well as lessons in academic subjects, so that mental and physical development are stimulated at the same time.

During adolescence the child undergoes changes in his psychological make-up as important and significant as those in the first five years of life. During this period between the dependency of childhood and the freedom of adulthood, the physical, social, and emotional changes that occur sometimes cause dramatic open conflict between the adolescent, his parents, and society. This, of course, is not true of all teenagers, and many youngsters ripen into adulthood with little or no difficulty.

Adolescence is frequently described as 'the awkward age', but in point of fact there is generally no loss in physical skill or coordination. Tests of physical skills, muscular coordination, and athletic ability show a steady increase in ability during the transitional years. Why then do adolescents appear to be so uncoordinated and incompetent? Perhaps it is because we expect them to behave like the seventeen- or eighteen-year-olds that they in part resemble, rather than the twelve- to sixteen-year-olds that they are. Adjustment expresses itself in various forms. The more noticeable problems are insufficient skill and knowledge in making the appropriate responses to different situations. In the past, parents, teachers, and other adults were in a position of greater authority than today; now the greater freedom and independence allowed to the adolescent by society increases his uncertainties. How does one ask a girl out to a dance? When should one plan to meet her family? A girl living alone or sharing a flat produces a situation that can be awkward for both boy and girl. These are very real problems to the adolescents and they will make mistakes in the process of growing up and learning. In full-time employment, an entirely new experience, the teenager has to learn a novel set of approved manners and behaviour. This uncertainty about what to do is reflected often in inconsistent work and expressions of great fatigue. Part of the time there may be intensive concentration and effort to get on with the job, but at other times the young worker may relax into childish pranks and irrational activities. Smoking, the wearing of adult clothing and cosmetics, vigorous debate about practical and theoretical issues, all are part of the process of development into adulthood. Some may make exaggerated efforts to pass as adults, while others may cling to their lost childhood and dependence Interest in the opposite sex and the desire to avoid conflicts and problems result in a new set of difficulties. The sex problem in Western civilization is created in part by the conflict between physical readiness for adult sexual behaviour and the cultural prohibition of intercourse before marriage. Other cultures may have formal initiation ceremonies in which the child is publicly and formally inducted into the adult society. The ceremonies may be painful but the transition period is short, and little of our modern uncertainty about behaviour is found in those cultures.

If a single word were needed to characterize adolescence it would be 'freedom'. The problems of this age are quite similar to the problems faced by new nations or former colonies which are obtaining independence. They want to be treated like adults and also wish the parent to have tolerance for their efforts to be individualistic, regardless of the consequences. The transition is made most smoothly if the change is anticipated and provisions are made through which the child naturally assumes more and more independence.

To help themselves over the uncertainties and the feelings of insecurity that permeate this stage of life, teenagers have found that grouping together is an aid to self-protection and psychological self-preservation. There is strength and sympathy and comradeship among members with the same problems.

These groupings, formal or informal, may result in common mannerisms, like choosing to wear the same type of dress, having the same style of haircut, participating in the same activities, admiring the same pop idols. Fortunately, almost all adolescents, in every generation, overcome their difficulties, aided by effort and understanding on the part of their parents (all former adolescents!) and grow up to be normal adult members of the community.

From *Psychology for Everyman* by Larry S. Skurnik and Frank George

TOGETHERNESS

Chinese young people cheering at a Peking rally

by Sven Oredson

At a peace rally: youths pursue a member of a rival group

Behaving Like Apes?

Chimps apparently live in troops of between 20 and 50 animals. Within these troops they form small groups of varying composition; the most basic group consists of females or females plus offspring. Adult females spending much time together often turn out to be mother and daughter, or sisters. Mother and offspring live together consistently, at least for the first four or five years of life, longer than in any other primate except man. During this time the young learn from their mother and from other chimps all the complicated acquired behaviours of chimpanzee adult life. Life for the young chimpanzee is relaxed and tolerant, and an infant will spend much of its time playing with other infants, with its mother and with its brothers and sisters. After this five year initial period, contacts with the mother are still maintained, particularly by daughters. Even sons return from time to time from their wanderings to greet their mothers affectionately.

. . . In the forest chimps are predominantly fruit-eaters (upon occasion they are cannibalistic!), but in open woodland they may add more protein to their diet. Males sometimes kill colobus monkeys or bush-pig; often males will gang up in a group to achieve their ends. Meat is a very choice item in chimpanzee diet and is eaten slowly and deliberately with a mouthful of leaves between each bite. It is sometimes shared out with other chimps who will beg for pieces. This food-sharing is very unusual among non-human primates; mostly it is every primate for himself. When the season is right chimps in woodlands also eat termites, and they do this by 'fishing' for them. When beginning a bout of termiting, an animal will carefully select stems or pieces of grass, trim them to the appropriate length, collect enough of them, and set out on the hunt for insects. It may pass over several termite hills if they are not ready and go on until it finds a mound ripe for fishing. Using a finger, a hole is scraped and the prepared twig inserted. Withdrawn covered with termites, it is passed carefully over the lower lip until every delicious morsel is removed, and the operation repeated. Clearly, in doing so, chimps are taking natural objects, modifying them to a standard pattern and using them for an objective which involves planning and forethought. They are, in fact, making tools. This has surprised many people, for previously man was considered to be the only tool-maker. In the chimpanzee, however, the intellectual abilities necessary for purposeful tool-making are already developed at an infra-human level. Other examples of chimp tool-use in natural surroundings have also been seen. For instance, chewed leaves are used as sponges to soak up water from holes in trees. They are also used to wipe dung or mud from the body. Stones and branches are used too in agonistic displays or when an animal is excited. They may be thrown under- or over-arm, often with considerable force and accuracy. Similar behaviour has been observed in other apes. Stones are used to open nuts too.

There are some further peculiarities of ape behaviour which are quite fascinating. Jane van Lawick-Goodall once observed a chimpanzee sitting, apparently transfixed, watching a beautiful African sunset. Can chimps have aesthetic tastes? Examples of ape art in zoos would suggest that this is certainly the case. In London Zoo chimps have learnt how to paint, always with a detectable individualistic style. They can match the compositional abilities of a three-year-old human child, before the first diagrammatic representation of the face. Painting is to a high degree 'autotelic', that is to say, self-rewarding. Ape painters hate being interrupted, even for food! Jane van Lawick-Goodall has also seen what she calls a 'rain-dance', an energetic and rhythmic series of movements performed by males, watched by excited females, when there is a tropical rainstorm.

From *The Evolution of Man* by David Pilbeam

Top: The daily chimpanzees' tea-party at London Zoo serves not only to divert visitors, but also to engage the chimpanzees' own considerable intelligence and so prevent boredom

Bottom: An orang-outang 'artist' at the easel

EVOLUTION ?

Some Key stages in the evolution of man, reconstructed from fossil remains. Left to right: Dryopithecus (Proconsul), an ape living some 20 million years ago, thought to resemble the common ancestor of apes and men; Australopithecus, who flourished about 2 million years ago and was probably the first toolmaker;

Pekin man (an example of Homo erectus), whose remains are about half a million years old; Neanderthal man, who occupied Europe for much of the last 100,000 years; Mount Carmel man, who lived 40–45,000 years ago, an early example of Homo sapiens; and Cro-Magnon man, anatomically indistinguishable from man today.

The aftermath of vandalism in a primary school

We're Grown-Up!

by Hans Ge Eriksson

at school

A research team interviewed 246 young men aged 14–20 living in Bethnal Green in East London. They were selected as being a reasonably representative cross-section of the young people living in the district. They were asked about the work they had done at school.

We asked the boys about the 'usefulness' of their lessons. Over half, both at school and at work, said the lessons were 'quite useful'. The general tone, however, was less complacent than this may suggest; most of the boys who said 'quite useful' did have complaints – 'Some of the subjects are a waste of time'; 'A lot of it was pointless.'

Despite the similarities in the proportions who were approving or critical of the various types of school, the comments varied markedly. The grammar schoolboys who spoke enthusiastically, for instance, often specifically mentioned the value of the G.C.E., as well as of their education more generally:

'You get a chance to ask questions at school and to find out things that would take an awful lot of time to find out for yourself. I assume I've got some intelligence, and the school can help you to use it – I got seven "O" levels, and I'm now preparing for my "A" levels. I think the school has given me a broader outlook on life as well – more of an appreciation of different things. And because of having a higher education, I can talk to all sorts of people.' (17, *grammar.)*

Present and former boys from comprehensive schools more frequently mentioned the vocational usefulness of their courses.

'I'm getting on all right at school. I want to be a draughtsman, and what we're doing at school is useful—it's all technical.'
(15, *comprehensive*.)

Some also mentioned more general benefits. An 18 year old, formerly at a mixed comprehensive school, said:

'For printing, which is what I went into, the technical lessons were very useful. The English helped me too – the way I speak – and, apart from the actual lessons, I learnt concentrating, which is useful.'

The secondary modern boys who felt their education useful to them usually made more modest claims for it. Some, like those from comprehensive schools, did talk about the value of technical courses – 'I want to be a tool-maker and they're teaching me how to make tools' (14 year old); 'The lessons were quite useful to me because in my job I have to do technical drawing and I need quite a lot of maths' (16 year old). More expressive of the general view taken by ex-secondary modern boys was the remark of one, now aged 20, who said, 'The lessons were useful for the type of brain we had – only basic English and basic arithmetic.'

Grammar school critics often mentioned, in particular, subjects they regarded as dead or out of date. 'What use is Latin to me?' said one boy. And another – 'I'll never be a Frenchman as long as I live, what's the use of me learning French?' Yet another – 'I'm not interested in reading Shakespeare or anybody like that; I'm just not interested because they're out of date. I haven't got much time for tradition or the past.'

The comprehensive and secondary modern critics also felt that much of their course was remote from life. But the complaint was not so much that the subjects were part of an out of date or irrelevant culture, though this was sometimes said. It was more often that the school simply provided no practical training. The secondary modern boys, particularly, complained that the lessons were of no use in their job.

'Most boys at my school, their attitude was this isn't going to help me when I leave school so I won't bother. The school didn't give you enough scope on trades – it was nothing to do with your job later on. Maths, history – all that crap; anyway half the time I didn't know what they were talking about, to tell you the truth.' (19, *ex-secondary modern*.)

Another former secondary modern pupil, aged 16, said about history:

'History was horrible; it drove you up the wall. He'd write something on the wall and you just had to take it down in your books. Bloody Napoleon and all that crap. We'd say, "We ain't got no interest in this," and he'd say, "Then you've got to find interest; it may come in useful to you." So I said, "I ain't leaving the country," and he said, "Don't you ever read the papers? Perhaps it will help you to read what's in there." Yes, he said all that junk would help you read the papers.'

A common theme among former and present secondary modern boys was that, in general, the school curriculum was dull or uninteresting.

'It's dreary, it's a drag. I'd like to get out to work and earn some money.' (15, *secondary modern*.)

'It was the same thing every day – dead boring, dead dull. I didn't pay much attention. It's just a laugh, really, because they never learned us nothing. Mostly it was a waste of time. I didn't go to school all that much, to tell you the truth. At one time I stayed away a bit too much, and the teacher said, "You'll have to shoot in a bit more often."' (17, *ex-secondary modern*.)

From *Adolescent Boys of East London* by Peter Willmott

Summerhill School

A. S. Neill, the founder of the school,
is on the bottom left

Summerhill was founded in the year 1921. The school is situated within the town of Leiston, in Suffolk, and is about one hundred miles from London.

Some children come to Summerhill at the age of five years, and others as late as fifteen. The children generally remain at the school until they are sixteen years old. We generally have about twenty-five boys and twenty girls.

The children are housed by age groups with a housemother for each group. The intermediates sleep in a stone building, the seniors sleep in huts. Only one or two older pupils have rooms for themselves. The boys live two or three or four to a room, and so do the girls. The pupils do not have to stand room inspection and no one picks up after them. They are left free. No one tells them what to wear: they put on any kind of costume they want to at any time.

When my first wife and I began the school, we had one main idea: *to make the school fit the child* instead of making the child fit the school.

I had taught in ordinary schools for many years. I knew the other way well. I knew it was all wrong. It was wrong because it was based on an adult conception of what a child should be and of how a child should learn.

Well, we set out to make a school in which we should allow children freedom to be themselves. In order to do this, we had to renounce all discipline, all direction, all suggestion, all moral training, all religious instruction.

My view is that a child is innately wise and realistic. If left to himself without adult suggestion of any kind, he will develop as far as he is capable of developing. Logically, Summerhill is a place in which people who have the innate ability and wish to be scholars will be scholars; while those who are only fit to sweep the streets will sweep the streets. But we have not produced a street cleaner so far. Nor do I write this snobbishly, for I would rather see a school produce a happy street cleaner than a neurotic scholar.

What is Summerhill like? Well, for one thing, lessons are optional. Children can go to them or stay away from them – for years if they want to.

The children have classes usually according to their age, but sometimes according to their interests. We have no new methods of teaching, because we do not consider that teaching in itself matters very much. Whether a school has or has not a special method for teaching long division is of no significance, for long division is of no importance except to those who *want* to learn it. And the child who *wants* to learn long division will learn it no matter how it is taught.

Children who come to Summerhill as kindergarteners attend lessons from the beginning of their stay; but pupils from other schools vow that they will never attend any beastly lessons again at any time. They play and cycle and get in people's way, but they fight shy of lessons. This sometimes goes on for months. The recovery time is proportionate to the hatred their last school gave them. Our record case was a girl from a convent. She loafed for three years. The average period of recovery from lessons aversion is three months.

All the same, there is a lot of learning in Summerhill. Perhaps a group of our twelve-year-olds could not compete with a class of equal age in handwriting or spelling or fractions. But in an examination requiring originality, our lot would beat the others hollow.

A few years ago someone at a General School Meeting (at which all school rules are voted by the entire school, each pupil and each staff member having one vote) proposed that a certain culprit should be punished by being banished from lessons for a week. The other children protested on the ground that the punishment was too severe.

Summerhill is possibly the happiest school in the world. We have no truants and seldom a case of homesickness. We very rarely have fights – quarrels, of course, but seldom have I seen a stand-up fight like the ones we used to have as boys. I seldom hear a child cry, because children when free have much less hate to express than children who are downtrodden. Hate breeds hate, and love breeds love. Love means approving of children, and that is essential in any school. You can't be on the side of children if you punish them and storm at them. Summerhill is a school in which the child knows that he is approved of.

In Summerhill, everyone has equal rights. No one is allowed to walk on my grand piano, and I am not allowed to borrow a boy's cycle without his permission. At a General School Meeting, the vote of a child of six counts for as much as my vote does.

But, says the knowing one, in practice of course the voices of the grownups count. Doesn't the child of six wait to see how you vote before he raises his hand? I wish he sometimes would, for too many of my proposals are beaten. Free children are not easily influenced; the absence of fear accounts for this phenomenon. Indeed, the absence of fear is the finest thing that can happen to a child.

From *Summerhill* by A. S. Neill.

Photographs by John Walmsley
from *Neill and Summerhill*

Girls' Magazines Then...

FIRST PART OF NEW VOLUME.

Part 58.—Nov., 1884.] Containing the Numbers for October. [Price 6d.

THE GIRL'S OWN PAPER

Coloured Frontispiece : **DREAMING.** From the Picture by M. ELLEN EDWARDS.

Mongolian Girls: How they Live and What they Look Like. By the Rev. JAMES GILMOUR, M.A., Author of "Among the Mongols."

Flowers of Joy and Sorrow. A Poem. By F. B. DOVETON.

How I Keep House on £250 a Year. By MARY POCOCK.

How to Make a Metronome.

On Emigrating as Domestic Servants to New Zealand.

Varieties.

A Memory. A Poem. By SARAH DOUDNEY.

For Listeners at Instrumental Concerts. 1. The Strings of the Orchestra. By JAMES MASON.

Honour Thy Father and Thy Mother; or, the Duties of Girls to their Parents, Guardians and Employers. By SOPHIA F. A. CAULFEILD.

Birthday Roundels. By C. G. FURLEY.

Friendship. By A. C. DUTT.

The Penalty of Riches.

A Work of Love. A Letter from the LADY BRABAZON.

Useful Hints.

The Fairies. A New Pianoforte Piece. By ERNST PAUER.

Dreaming. A Poem.

Imitation Barbotine Painting upon China. By BLANCHE C. SAWARD.

Poultry as Food, and How to Cook it. By PHILLIS BROWNE.

Father's Slippers. A Poem. By WILLIAM LUFF.

Notices of New Music.

The Queen Bee.

The Girl's Own Home. Subscription List.

Dress : In Season and in Reason. By A LADY DRESSMAKER.

Our Fraternal Society. The Cruet-stand and its Contents. By DORA HOPE.

Toydonia; or, the Land of Toys. By EMMA BREWER.

Our New Prize Competitions.

Answers to Correspondents.

COMPLETE STORY—**Far Above Rubies.** By ISABELLA FYVIE MAYO.

NEW SERIAL STORIES

The Mountain Path. By LILY WATSON, Author of "Within Sight of Snow."

Seven Years for Rachel; or, Welsh Pictures Sketched from Life. By ANNE BEALE, Author of "The Queen 'o the May," etc.

The Illustrations in this Part are drawn by M. ELLEN EDWARDS, JOHN CHARLTON, EDWARD WHYMPER, G. H. EDWARDS, R. CATTERSON SMITH, A. FORESTIER, FRANK CARLESS, BLANCHE C. SAWARD, JOHN DINSDALE, SUSAN R. CANTON, and others.

London: 56, Paternoster Row,
AND OF ALL NEWSAGENTS,

Contents bill of *The Girl's Own Paper*, 1884

...And Now

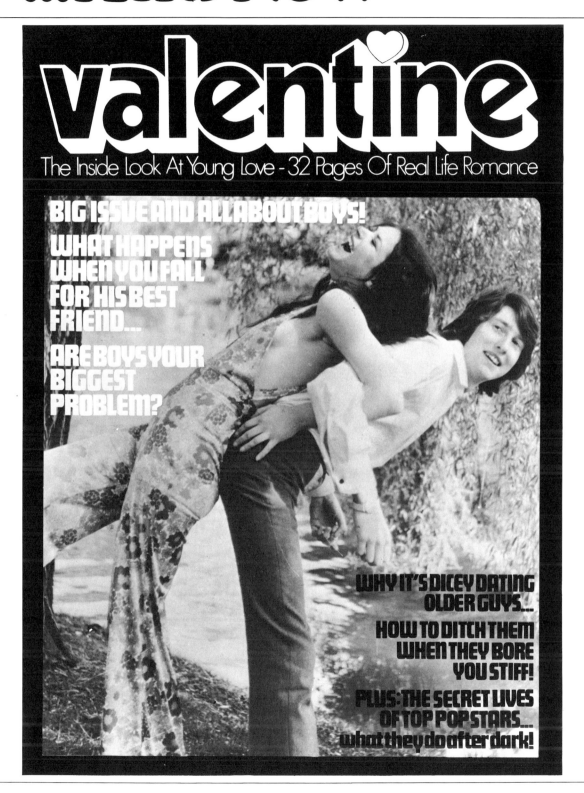

valentine

The Inside Look At Young Love - 32 Pages Of Real Life Romance

BIG ISSUE AND ALL ABOUT BOYS!

WHAT HAPPENS WHEN YOU FALL FOR HIS BEST FRIEND...

ARE BOYS YOUR BIGGEST PROBLEM?

WHY IT'S DICEY DATING OLDER GUYS...

HOW TO DITCH THEM WHEN THEY BORE YOU STIFF!

PLUS: THE SECRET LIVES OF TOP POP STARS... what they do after dark!

YOUNG PEOPLE AT THE TURN OF THE CENTURY

...And Now

A fifteen-year-old pupil at Tonbridge School, Kent, registers his protest against his headmaster's policy on long hair. The headmaster said he had written to parents asking them to make sure their boys' hair was clear of the collar at the back and of the eyebrows in the front.

From *The Times Educational Supplement*

By Rudi Herzog

Agonies of Adolescence

Being a teenager can be miserable and the compensations are meagre if you've a chinful of pimples or you're bursting out of your clothes with puppy fat. To begin this week's Young Observer, CHRISTINE DOYLE our medical correspondent takes a consoling look at the plight of the adolescent.

One girl wrote recently to a student organisation with a desperate plea for advice on plastic surgery, saying that without help she might kill herself. Another girl saved up for plastic surgery on her nose from the age of 11. It was only when she was 16, and a boyfriend told her she had the most beautiful nose he had ever seen, that she spent her money on something else.

The shape of a nose and hundreds of problems like it have always been the private worries and agonies of adolescents. A random check around any group of apparently well-adjusted and successful adults would produce a classic list of hang-ups.

There are those who had appalling spots – though some doctors believe that today there are fewer of these about (possibly because teenagers take great pride in their long hair and wash it fairly often).

There are those who wept all day when they learnt that they would have to wear glasses permanently; the women whose adolescent bosoms never seemed to develop, no matter how many exercises accompanied by chants of 'I must, I must, I must improve the bust' they carried out. One now distinguished reporter worried desperately about her red nose; another felt his whole life ruled by a stutter; many despaired of adolescent podginess, yet had to eat up all the good but stodgy food set in front of them.

A six-foot teenage boy suffered years of embarrassment in enforced short pants, being giggled and laughed at by the 'girls in Woolworths'; others hated being with their parents in front of their friends; some worried about their voices breaking, one being in agony because it seemed years before he could make himself heard above the slightest noise.

Parents were loathed for talking about children in front of their friends – and even worse laughing at their stupidities; some longed for the assurance to converse on equal terms with their parents' friends; others recall self-consciousness, shyness and blushing. One particularly remembered his resentment at his parents' reluctance to spend just enough on his clothes to keep him at least in fashion if not madly up-to-date.

There were desperate secret worries as to whether they were normal sexually. Did hero-worship of an older girl or boy mean they were homosexual or lesbian? Should you masturbate? What was the length of an average penis? There were the innumerable terrors of first going out with boys or girls. What did you say? How far did you go? Was it true that Tom, Dick or Harry really did do what he said he did? Would the other girls laugh, be jealous or talk about you? A major fear for girls was being given 'a bad name'.

Women recall their bitterness at never being allowed to stay out late when the rules for their brothers seemed quite different; convent girls railed against their inhibited preparation for life – 'Beware corrupting influences and don't get into bad company', but you had to find out just the same.

Most of today's teenagers share identical or very similar worries. One doctor, for instance, writes that there is still an extraordinary amount of shame associated with masturbation, even though many more people now regard it as a normal stage of sexual development – not 'You will grow out of it' as though it were something very immature, but 'You will grow into something else', so that masturbation becomes 'redundant'.

However adolescents nowadays do face other difficulties.

Drugs, for instance. Even to people now in their late twenties drugs in their adolescent days were very firmly doled out for an illness only or were associated with an unattractive and very distant fringe of heroin addicts. There was talk of people taking an occasional stimulant to help them through finals, and writing their name over and over again on their examination paper. But no one knew for sure, and it would be a rare student who had any idea where you could get hold of 'drugs'.

Today, pills and pot are freely available. Teachers like to think that 'it doesn't go on in my school', but, according to at least one survey, any student knows where he can get a supply of whatever he might want to experiment with.

Then there is the Pill. Birth control is safer, and we are told that because of it women have been sexually emancipated. Society generally is less horrified by the idea of pre-marital sex relations, and is gradually becoming much more sympathetic to unmarried mothers. Yesterday's teenagers were warned off anything 'worse' than a loving kiss, as though it were shameful and unhealthy unless one was married. And, of course, we now have the Abortion Act so that 'mistakes' can be put right.

There are other differences. Teenagers have more money and a well established youth culture – clubs, clothes, magazines, music. They do not, as did many teenagers only 12 years ago, emulate their parents – in their dress, for instance. The family as a unit is becoming much less close-knit, and the tribe system is weaker, so that both physically and emotionally teenagers are on their own much sooner. And they are perhaps more conscious than their parents were when they were teenagers that adults are creating an increasingly insecure world.

Many of these changes mean that the range of possibilities open to teenagers is now much wider. There are more decisions to be taken. 'Do you or don't you take drugs?' 'Do you or don't you sleep with your boyfriend or girlfriend?'

Adults sometimes think that teenagers of today with their way-out gear and rebellious behaviour, are, compared with their own youth, bizarre, if not unnatural or delinquent. Yet, basically, teenagers are no 'new race'. They are simply doing what every other generation of teenagers has had to do – move from the fixed rules of childhood, when things were decided for them, and establish a base from which to operate in the adult world.

From *The Observer Magazine*

Schoolgirls see the future boss as 'Prince Charming'

By *JOHN IZBICKI, Education Correspondent*

A GROUP of 14-year-old girls, asked by their teacher to write about " My first day at work," turned in an essay like " the last act in a pantomime with the managing director cast as Prince Charming," Mrs Barbara Bullivant, secretary to the Confederation for the Advancement of State Education, says in an article published today.

She says that children as well as parents should be given far more and better careers advice by schools.

In the article which forms part of the National Union of Teachers' annual guide to careers, Mrs Bullivant says the girls' essay showed exactly how unrealistic their idea of work was.

The managing director was seen " coming down the steps to welcome the new office girl, to lead her by the hand to her office and to introduce her to all the charming people she would be working with."

Important decisions

The main aspects of education, health and careers, are to many parents " the main reason for having schools at all," says Mrs Bullivant. Some large schools were not doing all they could in giving proper careers guidance.

" I heard recently of a class of 13-year-old girls who were gathered together in the hall one Monday morning and told they must decide whether or not they wished to continue to study French.

" Their answers were to be ready by mid-morning. Parents were not informed about these decisions, even after they were made.

" No 13-year-old should be left to make such important decisions without the guidance of both teachers and parents."

Forms sent home to demand such a choice were not good enough either. Parents had to be told about which options to keep open and which doors would be closed if certain subjects were dropped.

Mrs Bullivant, a mother of four, urges that children should be told about further, higher and adult education in their first year in secondary school. " The school must explain to the pupils what it is doing and what education is about."

The first days in employment can be " a shattering experience" because young people are then considered grown up. They cannot easily " express disappointment, boredom and fear."

But those who had been " well prepared at school and are well supported at home, will get over this time more easily."

From *The Daily Telegraph*

Away from home

Photographs by Timothy Couch

LONDON

London

    crossfigured
    creeping with trams

and the artists on sundays
             in the summer
all 'tracking Nature'
           in the suburbs
  It
    could have been anyplace
      but it wasn't
        it was
          London

        and when someone shouted over
that they had got a model

      I ran out across the court

    but then
      when the model started taking off
her clothes
      there was nothing underneath
          I mean to say
she took off her shoes
      and found no feet
    took off her top
      and found no tit
      under it

and I must say she did look
      a bit
      ASTOUNDED

      just standing there
      looking down
    at where her legs were
        not

But so very carefully then
        she put her clothes back on
and as soon as she was dressed again
        completely
    she was completely
      all right
  Do it again! cried someone
      rushing for his easel

But she was afraid to

      and gave up modelling

and forever after

      slept in her clothes

Lawrence Ferlinghetti

ON THE WAY TO WORK

FIRST DAY AT WORK

Photographs by Jacqueline Allwood

'Go and get a new bubble for my spirit level, a
couple of large sky hooks, a left-handed screwdriver,
and a long wait.'

HAPPY AT WORK?

" IF YOU LAYABOUTS DON'T GET DOWN TO A BIT OF HARD WORK YOU'LL LAND UP ON AN ASSEMBLY LINE , AS UNSKILLED WORKERS. THAT MEANS £40 CLEAR A WEEK, WITHOUT OVERTIME, BUT YOU WON'T GET A PENSION — OR THAT INNER SPIRITUAL HAPPINESS THAT A REAL VOCATION GIVES YOU . "

by David McKee

The research team, working as described on page 28, asked young men in Bethnal Green how satisfied they were at work.

Once at work, how content were the boys with their jobs? We put some specific questions about attitudes to work; whether the boys were satisfied or dissatisfied with their job in general, with the pay and with the prospects, and what sort of work they first 'expected' and second would 'choose' to be doing in future.

The answers to the first three questions, as far as they go, suggest a fairly high degree of 'satisfaction'. About four fifths of the boys said that they were 'satisfied' with their job generally; just over two thirds with the pay; nearly three quarters with the prospects. Most of the rest said they were 'dissatisfied'; on prospects, two boys gave 'in-between' answers – 'so-so', 'difficult to say' – and one did so on his job generally. So the level of contentment was apparently high. In talking about the future – we asked them about the prospects ten years ahead – half said not only that they expected to be doing the same kind of work but also that they would 'choose' to.

There were no marked differences in their answers on most of these questions in terms of the kind of job they had, the district they worked in, whether they were apprentices or not, or the kind of school they had gone to. One exception was that the 'higher' the status of the job, the more likely were the boys to describe themselves as 'satisfied' with their prospects; 80 per cent of the boys in non-manual said that they were 'satisfied', compared with 73 per cent in skilled manual work and 62 per cent in semi-skilled or unskilled.

It is obvious that to ask the boys whether they were 'satisfied' – with pay, prospects or their job generally – could provide only a crude measure of their attitudes. In fact, most were neither completely 'satisfied' nor 'dissatisfied'; they generally liked some aspects of their job but not others. It is clear, too, that boys can 'like' their job in different ways. Some meant that they got satisfaction from exercising their skill, others that they found the job tolerable or that they liked the other people there. Some laid more emphasis on their present feelings about their work, others on its prospects for their future. In all this there seemed a different emphasis between boys in different types of occupation.

Among some boys in skilled jobs, the skill itself gave pleasure.

'Arrived at the firm at 7.55. Sat down at my bench and started repairing a pair of Georgian candlesticks which were made in the year 1759 by James Gould. First I took the bottom off and then ran the rosin out of them. Then I burnt them out and pickled them – pickle consisting of eight parts water and one part sulphuric acid. I left them in the pickle for about fifteen minutes and then rinsed them under water and dried them out. Then with a colet hammer I tapped the bruises out of them and burnished them. Then, using easyflow flux and easyflow solder, I filled in the holes and pickled them again to remove the flux. I went to dinner at one o'clock in the café across the road, and returned to work at 1.30 p.m. Then I got the candlesticks out of the pickle again and filed them up, filled them with rosin and sent them down for sanding and polishing ready for plating. My last job was to sort out some elephant feet ready for the next day – we make all sorts of things out of them, such as umbrella stands, decanters, waste-paper bins. At 4.50 p.m. I had a wash and I left work at five o'clock.' (19, *silversmith.*)

'Most of the people at the school I went to had an ambition to be bank clerks, doctors and things like that. But printing always fascinated me right from the beginning, and I made up my mind to go into it six months before I finished at school. It's very interesting – you're doing different things all the time, and one day a week I go down to the London College of Printing to learn more about the theoretical side of it. There's one machine in our firm that I'm really looking forward to working on when I get the chance. There are only two of them in the country, and most of the time people are coming in and looking at it. It's a kind of showpiece, four-colour work – you know, really good-class work.' (18, *printer, ex-grammar.*)

'I like the butchery trade very much. It gets you full of grease and it makes you smell a bit when you come home, but it's a good life – open air, you're in the shop and you meet people, it's really interesting, never monotonous. The most important thing about a job is getting to the top – mastering the whole lot. In this particular job it's not just cutting meat – you've got to take the veins out, you've got to know where the veins are.' (19, *kosher butcher.*)

There were other boys who said they were happy in their work, and who, though they did not expressly say so, gave the impression of enjoying the work itself as well as other aspects of the job. One was a 17-year-old fitter's mate who worked in a converted railway arch in Bethnal Green, now a garage.

'I'm happy there, I have a laugh. Everybody likes everybody else. I'll stay there as long as I can, as long as they'll have me. The only promotion I would want is to become a fitter; I'd be happy as a fitter. I'm underneath cars for about four out of every eight hours – putting in new clutches, axles, giving it a clean-up. Sometimes you lose your temper, but there's nothing you can do. And you get cheesed off having to wash so much when you get home from work. Some of my mates don't have to wash till next morning, but I have to take my boots off and get washed all over because of the grease. But I don't mind being dirty, as long as the money's there – the money's all right in this job. Sometimes when a job won't give way I lose my temper; and I walk away for five minutes and have a smoke. It's worse in the winter, the snow coming in your face, you're under a lorry, and you really just want to give up. Sometimes you get called out at night on a breakdown. In winter you can hardly feel your fingers; you think about the people in an office, it's so cold you wish you were in there. But if I had my time again, I'd do the same again.'

Prospects for the unskilled

More complaints about the lack of opportunities came from the boys with unskilled or semi-skilled jobs.

'I get a fair wage for what I do, but I'd like to better myself. There are really no prospects in my job. I'd rather be a tradesman – I don't like to sort of wait on other people. In ten years' time? I'd definitely like to have a trade in my hands by that time – or at least a semi-skilled trade. I think I'd like to be a carpenter or a joiner.' (18, *building labourer*.)

'It's not what I want – there are no prospects at all. I'll be doing the same job and earning the same amount of money when I'm about 30.' (17, *warehouseman*.)

Dissatisfaction was reflected in how often boys changed their jobs. In general, they did not change jobs much – nearly half (44 per cent) of those at work were still in the job they had first taken when they left school. But there were some who had a much less stable work-history and it is not surprising that they were more often in semi-skilled or unskilled work than skilled or non-manual, as the table shows.

Boys' occupation and number of jobs since school

Number of jobs	Non-manual	Skilled manual	Semi-skilled and unskilled manual
Four or less	85%	83%	65%
Five or more	15%	17%	35%
Total %	100%	100%	100%
Number	45	95	37

More than a third of the semi-skilled and unskilled boys – compared with a sixth of the others – had been in five jobs or more. The explanation for this difference is not simply that boys in less skilled occupations had generally left school earlier and therefore had more time to change jobs; among boys who had been at work for the same number of years, those in unskilled and semi-skilled jobs had consistently changed more often.

What this changing about can mean was described by a 17 year old who had held six jobs since leaving school at 15.

'When I left school I went down to the youth employment and told them I wanted to go in for a mechanic or something like that. They said I didn't stand a chance, and I've more or less done unskilled jobs ever since then. I've been looking for something better, but I can't seem to find anything. You get in a job and you know it's not for you. You dislike it and you're unhappy, and you try to find another job, but when you get to that you find it's just a labourer again. If you're not a tradesman you have to do any job that comes along, and when you're a labourer you just go to work and you're the underdog. You don't know any job, so you've got to do what someone else says. Sometimes it really gets you down to be told and told and told all the time. And then you look for something else and you find you're back at the same sort of thing all over again.'

A 20 year old recounted his experience.

'I stayed in my first job as a clothing salesman in a shop for about six weeks. I thought there'd be younger people there I could work with. They were all about 40 – middle-aged – I felt out of place. So I went into the Post Office until I was $17\frac{1}{2}$, and then I worked as a builder's labourer. Then I had some other jobs after that – the last job I had before this was at a builders' merchants – I didn't like the foreman, he had no patience, not only with me but with the customers too. I always used to get the needle about that. I packed it in. Now I'm at a radio and TV warehouse. I don't know whether I'll stay there – I think the most important thing about any job is comradeship. In my last year at school I didn't have a clue what I wanted to do. I didn't take up any apprenticeship because I had the impression that once you've done that you're stuck to that job for the rest of your life, and I didn't want to get tied up.'

Why had such boys not followed so many of their schoolmates into jobs where they could learn a skilled trade? The reason may have been that their school records were so poor that they would not have been accepted. Some gave a different explanation – either, like the boy just quoted, arguing that they had not been willing to surrender their freedom, or suggesting that they or their parents could not afford it.

'If you go in for an apprenticeship, you only earn about £5 a week until you're 21, and yet that's the best time of your life, isn't it, when you're young? I mean, I know people who're doing apprenticeships and they go to night classes every night, or they have to sit at home because they haven't got any money. I know your future's all right and all that, but you're not enjoying yourself, are you?' (17, *assembler*.)

'My family haven't got anything, and therefore I've got to have a job that suits the family, to keep them sort of thing as well as me. I mean, most boys who take these apprenticeships, their fathers have got a bit of money behind them. If they haven't got enough money to go out with at the end of the week, the father says, "Here you are, son, you go out and have a good time." Fellows like that, it's all laid on for them.' (18, *labourer*.)

These remarks often contained an element of envy and regret. Whatever their reason for not entering apprenticeships, the fact remains that these boys did lack a 'trade', did often drift from one job to another, did account for most of the rebelliousness and resentment about work.

At school, as at work, the boys could be broadly divided into those who were content, those who were moderately so, and those who rebelled. But how far do attitudes to school and work coincide? Are the 'rebels' at schools also those at work? If job-changing is taken as an index, it seems that there is an association. Of the 52 boys who were most critical of the school régime (as measured by their views on school 'rules'), less than a third were in the job they had when they left, against more than half of those sympathetic to the school. Similarly, nearly a third of the former, against just over a tenth of the latter, had been in five or more jobs. This is not simply a reflection of the relative instability of boys in unskilled and semi-skilled occupations: there was the same relationship between attitudes to school and number of jobs amongst non-manual and skilled manual workers.

The influence of age

So far the discussion of attitudes to work has ignored age. Do the boys' views change as they get older? Their answers to the trio of questions on their 'satisfaction' – with their job generally, with the pay and the prospects – suggest that they do. On all three indices of 'satisfaction', relatively few boys of 15 and 16 were 'dissatisfied' and relatively few, again, of 19 and 20. The most 'discontented' age was 17 and 18. The same conclusion was suggested by a closer examination of the few boys who were 'dissatisfied' on all three counts. There were only nine of them; eight of the nine were aged 17 or 18.

Why this cycle? It seems that, when boys first leave school, there is a 'honeymoon' phase. The boys who had not long left school revelled in their new independence: 'You have more freedom'; 'You're treated as an adult at work, not like a child'; 'It's mainly the money. You can stand on your own feet – don't have to keep running to Mum every time you want a couple of bob.' Later, the job is more likely to pall and excitement about 'independence' gives way to resentment at adult authority. But as the boys mature they apparently become more content with their lot. It may be that as they move into adulthood they are increasingly accorded adult status by their workmates. It may simply be part of a more general 'settling down' associated with courtship and the approach to marriage. It is worth noting, by the way, that there seems to be rather less 'acceptance' over 'prospects' than about the job 'generally' or about pay; presumably boys still in dead-end jobs at 19 and 20 have more reasons to be anxious.

There are three main conclusions from this chapter. The first is that most boys are – perhaps surprisingly – content with their work, though 'contentment' means different things in different sorts of job. The second is that there is a distinct chronological cycle, a movement in the direction of greater dissatisfaction and then back again towards reconciliation. Thirdly, age is not the only variable that matters: certain sorts of boy, in particular, are discontented with their job and resentful about it. They are predominantly in unskilled work (though by no means all in such jobs are unhappy); they change jobs often; they resent the authority of their superiors; and many of them are the same boys who disliked their schooling.

From *Adolescent Boys of East London* by Peter Willmott

Assembly line by Ray Dean

FACTORY TIME

I work in a factory. For eight hours a day, five days a week, I'm the exception to the rule that life can't exist in a vacuum. Work to me is a void, and I begrudge every precious minute of time that it takes. When writing about work I become bitter, bloody-minded and self-pitying, and I find difficulty in being objective. I can't tell you much about about my job because I think it would be misleading to try to make something out of nothing; but as I write I am acutely aware of the effect that my working environment has upon my attitude towards work and leisure and life in general.

My working-day starts with that time-honoured ritual known as 'clocking-in'. In a job such as mine this is one of the more constructive acts of the day. For the uninitiated: a lever is pressed and, in blue ink, a time is recorded on one's card. It's so mechanical that one expects the time to be always the same. But it isn't. Just have the effrontery to be late: then you will find that your time has been stamped in RED ink. The management may condone bad timekeeping, but that blasted clock seems to shed blood in anguish.

After clocking-in one starts work. Starts work, that is, if the lavatories are full. In an hourly paid job it pays to attend to the calls of nature in the firm's time. After the visit to the lavatory

there is the tea-break to look forward to; after the tea-break the dinner-break; after the dinner-break the 'knocking-off' time. Work is done between the breaks, but it is done from habit and is given hardly a passing thought. Nothing is gained from the work itself – it has nothing to offer. The criterion is not to do a job well, but to get it over with quickly. Trouble is, one never does get it over with. Either one job is followed by another which is equally boring, or the same job goes on and on for ever: particles of production that stretch into an age of inconsequence. There is never a sense of fulfilment.

Time, rather than content, is the measure of factory life. Time is what the factory worker sells not labour, not skill, but time, dreary time. Desolate factory time that passes so slowly compared with the fleeting seconds of the weekend. Monday morning starts with a sigh, and the rest of the working-week is spent longing for Friday night. Everybody seems to be wishing his life away. And away it goes – sold to the man in the bowler hat.

People who speak grandiosely of the 'meaning of work' should spend a year or two in a factory. The modern worker neither gives anything to work nor expects anything (apart from his wages) rom it. Work, at factory level, has no inherent value. The worker's one interest is his pay-packet. The accent on money is understandable – after all, we are shorter of it than most. In a factory basic wage rates are usually low. Not that the management can't afford to pay more: indeed, they do pay more – but not on the basic rate. Those last few £s that bring one a little nearer the elusive 'national average wage' have to be earned under pressure. By incentive schemes, piecework, bonus, merit-pay, call it what you will, the worker is introduced to the spirit of free enterprise competition. A wage to be earned becomes a prize to be won. Payment by results they call it. And the result of the results is yet another rise in the profits.

I help to make cigarettes. I also smoke them – I'm smoking one now. Each employee of the firm for which I work receives, from the age of 18, a free issue of cigarettes weekly. Initiation by gift. Personally, I'd prefer the money to the fringe-benefit, but it's the cigarettes or nothing. Admitted, I could sell the cigarettes, but I don't. So I smoke; even though I agree with the medical profession about the relationship between smoking and lung-cancer. Sometimes I feel as if I'm working in an arsenal, an arsenal full of noisy machines painted green – the colour of grass – attended by green-overalled women. My workmates know little and care less about the lung-cancer side of smoking. It's a long way from the tobacco factory to the coffin. So we keep churning them out, millions a day, converting the rather attractive raw material, parchment-like tobacco leaf, into unattractive cigarettes. We make a pittance, the company makes a fortune. Other drug pedlars go to prison.

It gets worse, too. Complicated new machinery doesn't make the worker's job any more rewarding: the effect is the opposite. Less, rather than more, skill is required. As machines grow more complex so they become more self-reliant. They need less looking after; and they get it. As automation increases productivity it also provides management with an excuse to cut down on labour. At first the workers object to a reduction in their numbers, but nearly always they eventually acquiesce; as things stand, they haven't much choice. So where one saw a man looking vacantly at two machines one now sees him looking just as vacantly at six. This may be a greater strain on his eyes, but it certainly doesn't give him any more responsibility or food for thought.

Though men are in charge of the machines, the actual operation of them is usually done by women. Sometimes there are as many as five women to a machine. In some departments the proportion of women to men is immense: yet supervision remains the prerogative of the male. The suffragettes didn't have much effect on the factory. The women are more talkative than the men; their topics differ, too. Where the men tend to moan about pay and conditions (but won't do anything about them), the women chatter all day long about their homes, their holidays, who's in the family-way and anything else unconnected with work. Women turn their minds from the futility of factory life. Maybe they are wise. Anyway, they are much happier than the men, and more independent. They are much more likely to ask for their cards. I'd ask for mine if I was a woman with a husband at work.

The factory in which I work overlooks a cemetery. Beyond the cemetery rows of sooty houses stretch to the horizon. The prospect from the factory window reminds me of a concentration camp. And yet this is where we live: this is where we are expected to find recompense for the pound of flesh we sell to industry. One might find it necessary to work in prison, but one should not be required to live in one.

Inside the factory the prospect is just as grim. To me, anyway, though the others seem not to notice it. The workers, that is. For management, of course, are ever willing to help in the division of labour. They recognize two categories of employee: staff and worker. It is more the type of job than the importance of the work that decides one's category. To work in an office is the passport to the élite. Although we are all employed by the same firm, the staff get more money, more pension, more sick-pay, more holidays, and work shorter hours, than the workers. The supervisor and the clerk are segregated from the mechanic by pay and conditions of work.

The staff are on the side of management. I suppose one could be radical in spite of one's job, but the staff know which side their bread's buttered on. Quite often the promotion of a worker to the staff is accompanied by a change of political allegiance. There is often a change of newspaper, too. No one, just no one, takes the *Daily Mirror* into the office. The *Express*, it seems, is O.K. More a change of punishment than of taste. The staff don't mix much with the workers, either at work or outside. They think they better maintain their image by contact with their own kind. They act superior, and the worker foolishly grants them deference.

By Dennis Johnson. From *Work*, edited by Ronald Fraser.

WORKMAN'S HAND

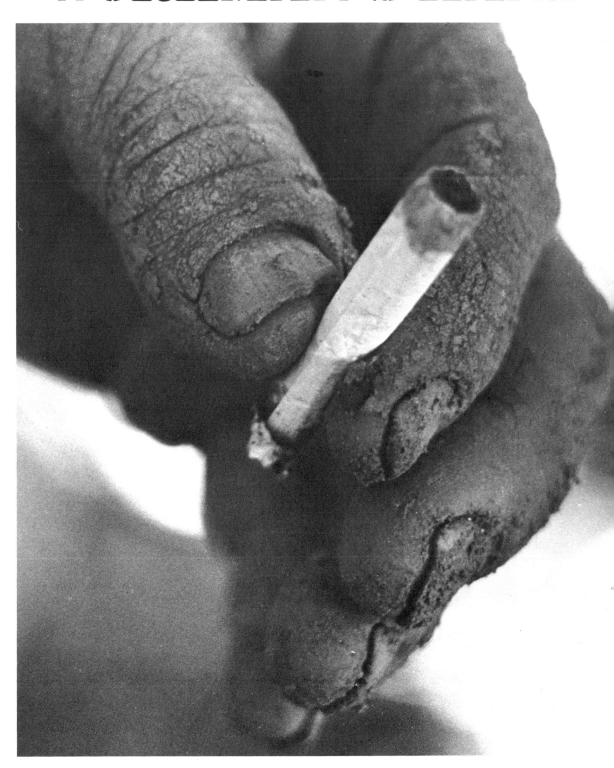

By Ulf Holmsted

THE CLERK

Start at the beginning: Civil Service Clerk, Temporary, at the local Ministry of Works depot in my home town. Can't get any lower than that. At the base of the bureaucratic pyramid, buried alive in fact, the temporary clerk is the navvy of the Civil Service, without status or security. When I took the job I'd only worked in factories, and so was a bit in awe of the office world I was about to enter. As an apprentice, queueing in the spotless corridor on Thursdays outside the Wages window, peering in at the comparative purity of desks and paper and slick dandified staff, you got a queer, dizzy sensation – something like Alice in Wonderland. My brother was a clerk himself, at the Council House, but I never connected him with this Thursday vision.

On my first day as a clerk, going down the street with my brother, I confessed how nervous I was. 'Listen,' he said, 'you can write your name can't you? You can add up? Then you can be a clerk.'

It was true. The depot was a big old house near the city centre, with the offices upstairs. My boss had a room at the front to himself, and behind him was a door leading to my den, which contained three others. This boss, a big, bumbling, embarrassed man addressed us all with the 'Mr' fixed firmly between, as if to maintain his distance. Everybody accepted his remoteness as inevitable, something which struck me as weird from the beginning, especially as you had to go to and fro behind his chair to the outer door every time you went to the lavatory, to the

foreman downstairs, to interview Irish labourers, and so forth. The boss sat through it all encased in silence and dignity, like an Under Secretary.

Holed up in the back room it was snug and at first I liked it, till the novelty wore off and the chronic, stagnant boredom began to take over. An old man, the only other Temporary, made tea in a corner where he sat, and he did all the menial labouring jobs, stamping and numbering time sheets, sorting vouchers: so at first I helped him. The other two did the more skilled entering and balancing, working on wage sheets, PAYE tabulations and other mysteries I never penetrated. It seemed to culminate, their activity, in the grand climax of pay day, which was Friday. Then the boss, for an hour or so, came out of his fastness and was nearly human. He'd march in smiling with the box stuffed full of money, and together they would count and parcel it. Out went the box again, stuffed with pay envelopes.

I ought to mention another clerk, who worked out in the boss's sanctum, I presume because of lack of space. I don't think he was higher in grade than the other two. Between him and the two in my place there was a non-stop cold war going on – I never found out why. The old man was treated with amiable contempt by the established clerks, who asserted their superiority now and again, and, as the old man was deaf, kept up a running commentary, half fun and half malice, which they evidently found necessary to break the monotony. Before long I needed it as much as they did. The worst aspect of a clerk's existence was being rubbed into me: it's how prison must be. At first you don't even notice; then it starts to bite in. Because of the terrible limitation on your physical freedom – *chained to a desk* is right – you are soon forced to make your own amusements in order to make life bearable. You have to liven it up. And with the constriction comes inevitably an undertow of bitterness, and all kinds of petty behaviour arise out of the rubbing frustration, the enforced closeness. Plenty of it is malicious.

In a factory, which I used to think was a bad enough prison, it is at least big enough for you to wander about physically and visit your mates on other sections. If you can stray from your desk as a clerk you're lucky, though it's true that no two office jobs are alike. The very worst kind, and they ought to be abolished, are those that have you lined up in rows facing the front, with the eagle eye on you and no excuse for moving at all. I had one exactly like that in a vast ordnance depot, Civil Service again, and the place of work was nothing more than a huge draughty shed with girder work in the roof and no ceiling. It held about fifty clerks, men and women, spaced out equally on a concrete floor at trestle tables, and all facing the glass box which contained the administrative staff. The boss in this fantastic set-up was a woman, and contact with this dragon – not that anybody wanted it – was impossible, unless you were on the mat for some crime. The jobs being done by all of us out on the floor were identical, as far as I could see. We had a pile of stores vouchers, a register, an indelible pencil each. There were numbers in your register which tallied with the vouchers. You had to find the corresponding number, tick a space, turn the voucher from a pile on your right to one on your left. No talking, no contact, nothing – unless you counted trips to the bogs. I had to move my legs somehow, just to convince myself I was still alive, so my trips became more and more frequent. When I wasn't squeezing out a drop of water I was washing my hands. I think I stuck it a week, then was hauled up in front of the dragon one morning for being half an hour late. I have never stumbled on such a nightmare since, and began to wonder if I dreamt it. How long could those others have been there, and why did they stick it? Monsters they must have been. When you find yourself amongst it, one of the damned like that, you don't pity your fellow victims, you loathe them. Somehow they get the blame for being there, for trotting in like sheep every day, for letting it exist. No doubt though it is still rotting merrily away, the whole shed-full.

Another clerical job, at a builders' merchants, was redeemed to some extent by the fact that you were actually in the warehouse, among storemen, sales reps, and all the tangible, fascinating paraphernalia of the trade, racks and bins and lofts stacked with it: one occupational hazard facing a clerk is always the sense of futility he struggles against, or is more often just overwhelmed by. Unlike even the humblest worker on a production line, he doesn't produce *anything*. He battles with phantoms, abstracts: runs in a paper chase that goes on year after year and seems utterly pointless. How can there be anything else other than boredom in it for him?

I admit that when I started in my first office job at the Ministry of Works, after years in a big factory, I liked it. For one thing it was much more human and relaxed, almost a family affair – even if the family got a bit testy now and then. I realize this was mainly a matter of size: working in a converted house with about twenty staff in it somewhere, as against 2,000 men in a great shed of machines and din, grinding in and out of the gates in herds, clocking in and out. Even the 'Mr' I enjoyed, though it made me feel daft. At least I was an individual again, not a number on a card.

But a really big office can be just as inhuman as a factory, you can punch a clock just the same, and the only real difference is your clean collar and alleged respectability. As for the idea that you're part of management, nobody is fobbed off with that guff any more. The only ones who want to believe it are the little bosses, the section heads on the climb up.

I work now in the engineering department of an Electricity Board. I am more or less given a free hand; as long as the routine stuff gets done and there are no complaints, nobody worries. It is an easy number, time to think and day-dream, congenial workmates, and I know from hard experience I'm not likely to find anything more pleasant. I'm not ungrateful. The basic fact remains though that, in common with the other jobs I've had, it has no value as work. It is drudgery done in congenial surroundings. You feel dispensable, interim: automation will take it over one day, the sooner the better. You are there for the money, no other reason.

By Philip Callow. From *Work*, edited by Ronald Fraser.

PEOPLE AT WORK

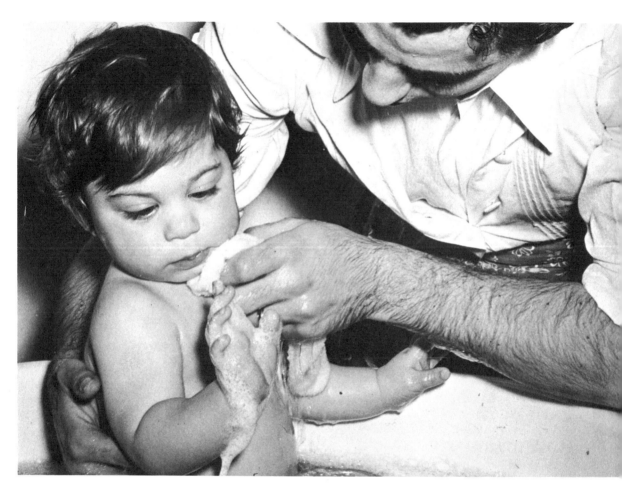

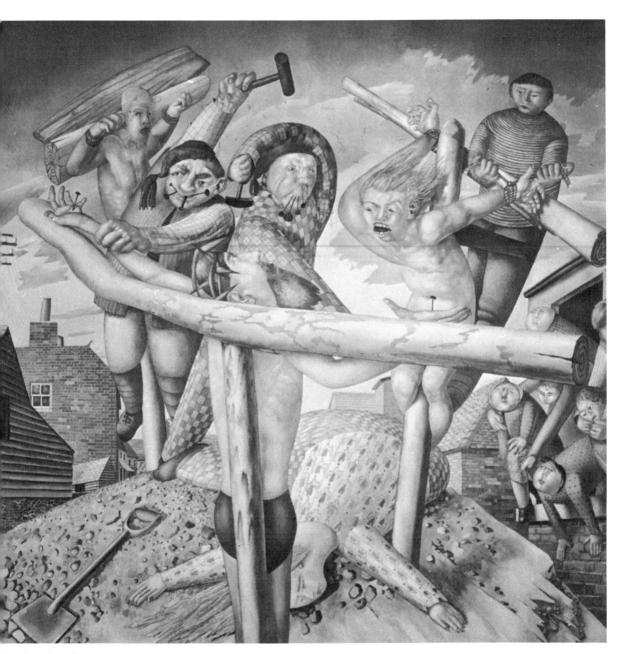

By Stanley Spencer

'Look at the man knocking in the nails. He's
just doing a job of work.' (Stanley Spencer)

YOUNG WORKERS GET TOO MUCH MONEY

Before the war it was common for parents to pay a premium for their son to be apprenticed, and most children earned barely enough for board and clothing. Today wages are such that many young people earn a substantial proportion of the wages they will ultimately earn as adults. Not infrequently it is more than that earned by their father or mother working full time. As a result of labour shortage, young people are able to change employment at a whim, and it is difficult for employers to exercise any discipline without losing an essential worker in a situation where any sort of labourer or machine minder is better than none. Many of the tasks required on machines and assembly lines are so simple that, in place of adults for whom a full rate has to be paid, employers can arrange to use young people at somewhat lower rates of pay.

The net result is that high wages are so easily earned that it is all too easy to have money, representing power and independence, without any sort of responsibility or discipline. Usually the mother is given a bare board and lodging contribution of about thirty to forty shillings and the rest is kept for clothes and amusement. This happens at a time when strong emotions, immaturity and inexperience render many young people incapable of exercising self-discipline and restraint.

The problem of these high wages is a very real one not only because of the immediate effects on the young people, but because the enormous spending power in the hands of impressionable, inexperienced and experience-hungry young people make them the target of very experienced, calculating, commercial interests who wish to transfer as much as possible of this wealth to their own organisations. It is only necessary to study the less reputable sections of the press and the advertisements for tobacco and drink to see that they aim at stimulating the animal emotions and making young people the mainstay of the tobacconist and the public houses in the future. It is hypocritical to cry out against the smoking habits, the drinking habits and the promiscuity of the young when such enormous stimulation is given which inevitably promotes the very faults which adult society hastens to condem.

It should be a primary responsibility of every parent to control the amount of spending money a young person of fifteen to eighteen should possess. An adequate sum should be deducted from the wage packet to pay for board and lodging. A weekly sum for pocket money to include clothes, holidays, and incidentals should be decided. The rest of the wages should be saved for the future. In present circumstances the facilities for saving in the Post Office, National Savings and Trustee Banks are such that no practical difficulty should be experienced in that direction. When young people marry at such an early age, as many of them do, there are few who could not have a substantial sum at their disposal if spending had been sensible and saving had been in proportion to their small responsibilities and large income. While acknowledging the difficulties of such a procedure one is inclined to advocate some compulsory form of teen-age saving.

This is of special importance at the present time when, because of high wages and small responsibilities, teen-agers possess an enormous aggregate of free spending money. This has been referred to earlier, but the market they represent is of great importance to commercial interests. These organisations will do everything in their power to create an artificial 'teen-age image' which will attract the interest of young people and tempt them to spend their money in ways profitable to the particular industry concerned. This may be smoking, drink, dress or adornment. The element possessing most attraction is sex and this is used ruthlessly in every form of advertisement and insinuated to focus interest in radio, television and press. It is fortunate that the young have a natural modesty and fastidiousness often lacking in adults who have had their values debased. In many of the media which form public opinion the good is ignored and the instincts which it is vital for society to control and guide into creative channels are wantonly exploited on the basest level.

From *Adolescence* by T. A. A. Hunter and M. E. M. Herford

Stimulating the Animal Emotions

PETER STUYVESANT

Discover a new world of fun and excitement. The wide and wonderful world of Peter Stuyvesant. King Size length of rich choice tobaccos. Special filter for that smoother flavour. Light up a Stuyvesant ...*You'll be so glad you did!*

The international passport to smoking pleasure

Six new pearls
from the Wild Pearl diver.

Pearls that bring a translucent sheen to your lips. Wild Pearl Lipsticks by Number Seven.

Now there are six new flattering shades to choose from. Delicately true colours that stay that way. Fresh non-staining colours with the opalescence of deep sea pearls.

Shades: Pale Lilac, Real Pink, Rose Beige, Mid Rose, Clover Pink, Warm Coral.

Wild Pearl BY NUMBER SEVEN

Available from Boots The Chemists.

Things happen after a badedas bath
(they say it's got something to do with the horse chestnuts)

badedas. Just a capful in your bath. Fantastic. Green waters which bubble like vintage champagne. Forget about soap. Just lie there. Be cleansed more kindly, more gently than you'd believe possible. Enjoy the mysterious action of a special extract of horse chestnuts.

The fresh smell of deep green continental forests.
And what happens afterwards? To the new, invigorated, re-born you? Quite simply. Lebenslust. Which the British, masters of under-statement, call joie de vivre.

badedas

the most stimulating thing since bathing itself-with extract of horse chestnuts

Valuable
(After reading two paragraphs in a newspaper)

ALL these illegitimate babies . . .
Oh girls, girls,
Silly little cheap things,
Why do you not put some value on yourselves,
Learn to say, No?
Did nobody teach you?
Nobody teaches anybody to say No nowadays,
People should teach people to say No.

Oh poor panther,
Oh you poor black animal,
At large for a few moments in a school for young children in
     Paris,
Now in your cage again,
How your great eyes bulge with bewilderment,
There is something there that accuses us,
In your angry and innocent eyes,
Something that says:
I am too valuable to be kept in a cage.

Oh these illegitimate babies!
Oh girls, girls,
Silly little valuable things,
You should have said, No, I am valuable,
And again, It is because I am valuable
I say, No.

Nobody teaches anybody they are valuable nowadays.

Girls, you are valuable,
And you, Panther, you are valuable,
But the girls say: I shall be alone
If I say 'I am valuable' and other people do not say it of me,
I shall be alone, there is no comfort there.
No, it is not comforting but it is valuable,
And if everybody says it in the end
It will be comforting. And for the panther too,
If everybody says he is valuable
It will be comforting for him.

Stevie Smith

From *Valentine*

THE SWEDISH ANSWER: UNISEX MARRIAGE

BY
SARA JOLLY
a British housewife who lived in Sweden for 3 years

WOULD you like a unisex marriage—with husband and wife sharing housework and breadwinning day and day about? I can only report that Swedish wives flourish on it.

They are outward-looking, and a conversation with them is likely to be about their work, hobbies or families. It is scarcely ever about what so-and-so said to offend them, or what women's place in society ought to be.

They are enthusiastic in all kinds of ways. During the three years I lived in Sweden while my husband was working there, I repeatedly heard how much Swedish wives appreciated and enjoyed their families and homes because they were away from them for some of the time in their own careers.

The average Swede, though tall and handsome, doesn't spend much time paying a woman compliments. Perhaps this is because he is quite prepared to treat her as an equal.

When a young couple marry they don't take it for granted that the husband is the breadwinner, and the wife the housekeeper.

They have a flexible approach, sharing out the work and chores in a way which suits them. No one criticises them if they reverse their traditional roles.

As Katerina, a Swedish wife, explained to me: "Stefan and I have known each other since childhood. We went to the same kind of school, and we both trained as dentists, so why should only one of us have a career?"

A doctor who works in a Child Care Department thought that women had a right to work and to support themselves.

"I can understand a woman who prefers housework to factory work, but I just cannot understand an educated woman who doesn't work."

"When we married I was studying," a woman psychiatrist told me. "And, of course, when I qualified I started to practise." She could not imagine training and then not using her vital skills.

Nor is it only professional women who expect to work. The girl who came to clean my house told me that her husband was a postman.

"He's up early, and then he comes home early in the afternoon and looks after the baby while I go out to work."

Increasingly, the Swedish husband accepts that household chores are partly his responsibility.

One working wife said: "I've never had to worry about housework. Whoever sees that something needs doing, does it. Perhaps I am a bit more interested in sewing, and my husband in the car, but we don't define any boundaries."

Another said: "My husband works three days and I work two. He cooks, cleans, baths the baby and looks after the children if they are ill, just as well as I do.

"We used to take the children to a neighbour while we were out working, but this way is much better for them."

She added: "We've streamlined the chores as much as we can. For instance, we buy all our food once a week and store it in the deep-freeze."

An architect's wife felt that her husband wasn't someone who cared about working flat out to reach the top of his profession at the expense of his family's happiness.

"We're planning that I will work a couple of days a week, and on those days Bjorn will work at home so that there is someone there when the children come home from school."

Wives who are not working tend to feel their lives lack something.

"Sometimes I ask myself what I've done with my life," said one. "I've brought up four boys—but so have lots of people."

Another confessed: "I feel so depressed sometimes. I have interests, but they don't seem enough. I almost envy my husband because he is so absorbed in his work and his hobbies."

From The Daily Telegraph

Home
Sweet Home

THE GOOD OLD DAYS

Writing about conditions in the early years of the nineteenth century among the bulk of the population which fell within the category of the 'labouring poor', J. H. Plumb comments:

The work was fifteen, or even sixteen hours a day, six days a week throughout the year except for Christmas Day and Good Friday. That was the ideal time-table of the industrialists. It was rarely achieved, for the human animal broke down under the burden; and he squandered his time in palliatives – drink, lechery, blood-sports.

It was impossible [he concludes] for most of them to live a life of more than bare subsistence and the natural disasters of their personal lives – unemployment, sickness, death of the bread-winner – left families in utter destitution, for the state had little conception of social service; its only answer for unemployment and poverty was the workhouse.

The conditions of life and work in the new factories, in the mines, and in the growing industrial towns were so unbelievably bad, by modern standards, that even to read about them is a harrowing and nauseating experience.

The working and social conditions of men, women, and children employed in mines were known to be deplorable long before the nineteenth century. Wesley, for example, writing of the people round Huddersfield in 1743, said: 'A wilder people I never saw in England. The men, women, and children filled the street as we rode along, and appeared just ready to devour us. Of the colliers in an area near Newcastle, he wrote that they were 'such as had been in the first rank for savage ignorance and wickedness of every kind'.

The report on Mines of 1842 revealed the conditions of employment in the mines in all their horrifying detail. At the age of six many girls spent the entire day in darkness attending to ventilation doors. Young boys, girls, and women dragged heavy loads of coal along passages to the bottom of the pit shaft. 'Chained, belted, harnessed like dogs in a go-cart, black, saturated with wet, and more than half naked, crawling upon their hands and feet, and dragging their heavy loads behind them – they present an appearance indescribably disgusting and unnatural,' wrote one commissioner in describing some examples of this kind of work. In some pits girls were working in passages no more than 26 inches high, and some adult women worked in passages no higher than 30 inches. The commissioner claimed that, in Lancashire, workers pulled their loads – often in passages no higher than 20 to 30 inches – for an average distance of four to six miles a day. In East Scotland girls and women between the ages of six and sixty or more carried to the surface of the pit, on their backs, burdens of coal varying in weight between $\frac{3}{4}$ cwt and 3 cwt. One woman, giving evidence, said that she made forty to fifty journeys a day to the surface carrying 2 cwt as her burden. 'Some females carry $2\frac{1}{2}$ to 3 cwt but it is over-straining.' The commissioner wrote: 'However incredible it may appear, I have taken the evidence of fathers who have ruptured themselves from straining to lift coal on their children's backs.'

Long hours of labour in such wretched conditions resulted in such desperate fatigue that time spent at home was chiefly time spent in recuperation. A woman working in the West Riding said: 'The work is far too hard for me; the sweat runs off me all over sometimes. I am very tired at night. Sometimes when we get home at night we have not power to wash us, and then we go to bed. Sometimes we fall asleep in the chair.' Many girls and women claimed that Sunday (their one day of rest) had to be spent in bed. Needless to say, physical deformities and diseases were common. The quality of family life of many mine-workers may be conjectured from the effects of the harsh conditions of work upon

Trolley-boys working underground

childbirth. Many women suffered distortions in the spine and pelvis which led to great difficulties in childbirth. Many pregnant women worked in the mines up to the day of the birth of their children. One woman stated that she 'had a child born in the pit' and brought it up the pit shaft in her skirt. Many said that a high proportion of the children born while they were in the pits were still-born.

It is, of course, impossible to generalize about the standards of morality of the people doomed to live in these wretched conditions, but it is feasible to suppose that among many members of the working population they were very low. Describing some of the districts of London later in the nineteenth century, the author of *The Bitter Cry of Outcast London* wrote:

'Marriage,' it has been said, 'as an institution, is not fashionable in these districts.' And this is only the bare truth. Ask if the men and women living together in these rookeries are married, and your simplicity will cause a smile. Nobody knows. Nobody cares. Nobody expects that they are. In exceptional cases only could your question be answered in the affirmative. Incest is common; and no form of vice and sensuality causes surprise or attracts attention. The vilest practices are looked upon with the most matter-of-fact indifference. The low parts of London are the sink into which the filthy and abominable from all parts of the country seem to flow. Entire courts are filled with thieves, prostitutes, and liberated convicts. In one street are 35 houses, 32 of which are known to be brothels. In another district are 43 of these houses, and 428 fallen women and girls, many of them not more than 12 years of age. A neighbourhood whose population is returned at 10,100 contains 400 who follow this immoral traffic, their ages varying from 13 to 50. . . .

Those who bemoan the immorality of the present day might ponder a little upon such an account of the past.

From *The Family and Marriage in Britain*
by Ronald Fletcher

69

HOW THINGS USED TO BE

An early promoter of pop music. In the early 1890's travelling pedlars sold song sheets.

Child labour in a Carolina cottonmill, 1908. By Lewis W. Hine *(George Eastman House Collection)*

Domestic servants before the
First World War

PLYMOUTH
EDUCATION COMMITTEE
PARENTS ARE REQUESTED
TO REMAIN OUTSIDE
THIS DOOR

A Plymouth school, 1969.

Your Country Expects...

Serving her country

Why Patriots are a Bit Nuts in the Head

Patriots are a bit nuts in the head
because they wear
red, white and blue-
tinted spectacles
(red for blood
white for glory
and blue . . .
for a boy)
and are in effervescent danger
of losing their lives
lives are good for you
when you are alive
you can eat and drink a lot
and go out with girls
(sometimes if you are lucky
   you can even go to bed with them)
but you can't do this
if you have your belly shot away
and your seeds
spread over some corner of a foreign field
to facilitate
in later years
the growing of oats by some peasant yobbo

when you are posthumous it is cold and dark
and that is why patriots are a bit nuts in the head

Roger McGough

Guernica. By Pablo Picasso. On 26th April, 1937, the little Spanish town of Guernica was razed to the ground by German planes, flying for Franco. The raid was intended to test the combined effects of explosive and incendiary bombs on a civilian population.

All Done in Sport

By George Doherty

Football hooliganism. A youth
is removed by the police during
demonstrations behind the
Liverpool goal.

Absurd Animal

Redder than holly are Mrs Mayhew's nails. They danced on the counter like circus riders' legs in red high-heeled boots. Her heels scraped the sawdust of the butcher's floor. The butcher put two pig's trotters in a bag and she gave him the money with a smile.

The pink dancers who first lay in the golden straw and later stood starred with mud in the rain, the double *pas de deux* of a running pig ended, wept blood in the paper bag.

Mrs Mayhew wore a polythene bag on her head to protect her home perm from the sleet but it ran down her face and neck and her red lips itched. She stood for shelter under Campbell the Butcher's awning, after venturing a few steps in the sleet. In the window a full-grown pig reclined on a bed of parsley. There was a sprig of parsley in either ear and one hung like a cigarette from the corner of his mouth.

'Mrs Campbell's ever so artistic,' thought Mrs Mayhew.

The table was laid for the evening meal and the potatoes were drained and hot trotters buttered. Mrs Mayhew looked at the green enamel clock – five o'clock.

Then she decided to go ahead with the meal. She heaped potatoes on her plate and added two pigs' feet to the pile. Wiping her lips with a Kleenex tissue, which she threw half-crumpled in an ashtray, she switched on the television and sat opposite it with a plate on her knee.

As she was eating a shadow flickered across the screen. She turned round just in time to see a pale snout-like face pass the window. Then the door opened. Mrs Mayhew screamed. A pig stood in the doorway on its hind legs. His front hooves were folded on his chest, his lower half was encased in a huge paper bag tied round the waist with string.

'I am looking for my feet,' he said.

When Mrs Mayhew came to she was lying on the floor. The television announcer was saying: '– And now we present *Pygmalion*.'

She looked at her plate: he had taken the potatoes as well.

From *Dust Falls on Eugene Schlumberger* by Shena Mackay

Factory Farming

The Advance of Science

Hitherto it has been usual for a child to be born of two parents of differing sex, both of whom were alive at the time of his/her conception. Such tedious limitations are rapidly disappearing, with unforseeable consequences for marriage and the family as we know it. Thanks to techniques for storing the male seed, it is already the case that a child may be conceived long after the death of the father. And a woman might bear a child to her great-grandfather one day. Indeed, research now in hand may make it possible for a woman to bear a child without male intervention, or even for a child to be born without the comfort of a maternal womb. The parents, if any, may be able to specify the sex of the child in advance, and even change it.

But these are simply advances in the single field of the reproductive process. In the field of ageing, gerontologists foresee both an extension of the life span and the preservation of a degree of youthful vigour into old age. Some even contemplate the possibility of immortality. Neurologists and others are exploring the brain, and hint at raising the level of intelligence, at improvement of memory and the control of moods and feelings. Geneticists are so confident of being able to tamper with heredity that they have begun to warn us to beware of them, while transplantation surgery has already begun to present us with ethical problems. Biochemists have even seriously proposed an attempt to synthesize life from inert materials. All these 'advances', it is evident, would have major social and ethical implications if they are really 'on'.

The difficulty which a writer faces in writing about such developments is that a general statement conveys only a feeble impression of the potentialities of the advance, whereas a concrete one appears hopelessly sensational and even repellent. Thus if I say that grafting techniques may make body parts completely interchangeable I suggest little more than a medical advance. On the other hand, if I say that one day someone might say to you, indicating another person, 'I want you to meet my uncle and niece. They were in a car smash but fortunately the surgeon was able to get one complete body out of the undamaged bits', I am more likely to evoke incredulity than alarm.

I suspect that the immediate reaction of many people to such forecasts is that, if not downright impossible, they lie so far in the future as to be o no practical importance to people now living. Nothing could be farther from the truth, I regret to say. While some of the possibilities hinted at by biologists, such as the attainment of personal immortality, may lie a century or more in the future, it is certain that much of what they are doing will begin to bear fruit in the lifetime of those now living.

. . . A primary difficulty in devising plans to meet the problems which biology is conjuring up is constituted by the fact that we have no clear or agreed idea of what kind of world we want. No doubt most people would vote for a social pattern much like the one they know, but devoid of its principal abuses. In the east, this would mean a world of cars and factories and Coca-Cola, without delinquency, ulcers, air pollution or crime. But investigation discloses that the advantages and disadvantages are reciprocally connected. We have air pollution precisely because we have cars and factories to produce goods. We have ulcers because we have a highly competitive productive system which monopolizes the bulk of the time of the bulk of the population. We have delinquency because this kind of footloose society, with its unrestricted communications systems, weakens family control of the young. And so on.

The statements, of course, are mere headlines with which I seek to outline great areas in an attempt to establish a point of view. The actual causes of delinquency, for instance, are complex and it is not my intention to over-simplify them. My point is the large one that all the features of a given society are functionally interconnected, and one cannot change one in isolation from the others.

If, then, we ask ourselves what kind of a society to aim for, on the assumption that we might make a radical change in the pattern, we find ourselves faced with a series of questions to which there are at present no quantitative answers. For example, at what level should we set the density of population so as to avoid either ndue isolation or disagreeable overcrowding? Or again, to what extent should we be willing to sacrifice the quality of the environment in order to consume goods? We are busy creating a world in which it is steadily easier to consume goods than to take our pleasure in the form of privacy, a low pace of work, communion with nature, or doing a job which one enjoys.

Current indications are that the world is bent on going to hell in a handcart, and that is probably what it will do.

From *The Biological Time Bomb*
By G. Rattray Taylor

River pollution. These are dead fish.

Just Around The Corner

▶ This research prototype of a four-legged quadruped machine, fabricated by General Electric Company engineers under a U.S. Army contract, was designed to spur development of equipment that will improve the mobility and materials-handling capabilities of the foot soldier under the most severe conditions. By means of an advanced control system, the machine mimics and amplifies the linear movements of its operator. The right front leg of the unit is controlled by the operator's right arm, its left front leg by his left arm, its right rear leg by his right leg, and its left rear leg by his left leg. The research prototype is 11 feet high and 3,000 pounds in weight.

▼ The new image of British Rail?

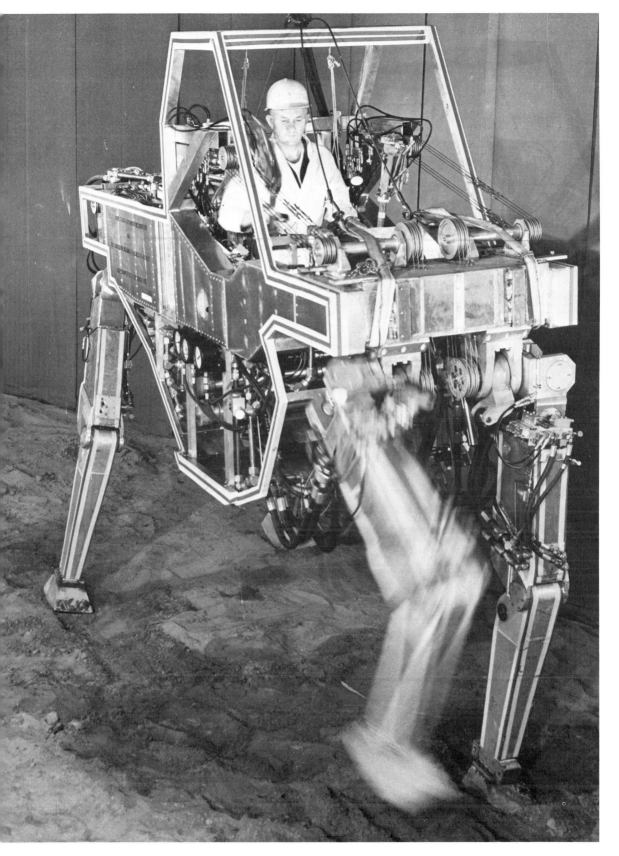

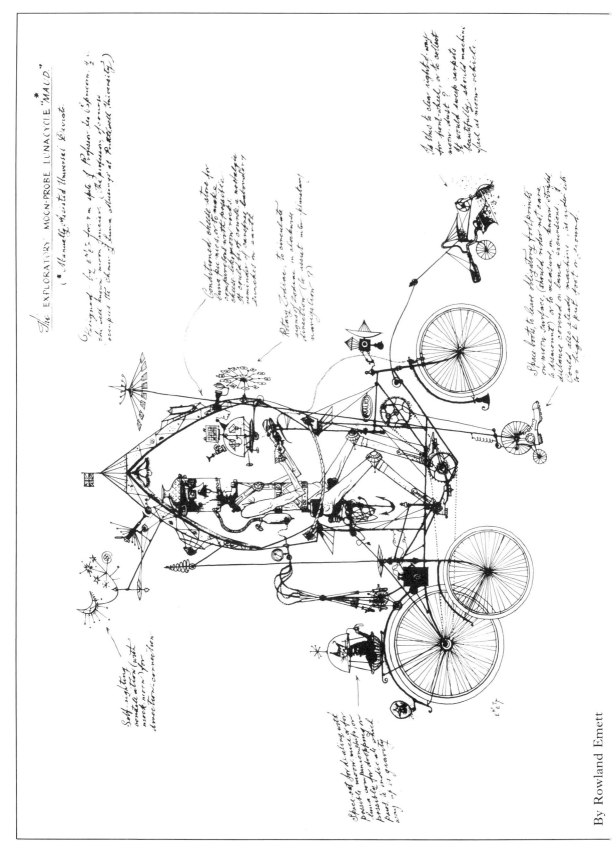

By Rowland Emett

Inventor Rowland Emett with his Lunacycle

No Morning After

'But this is terrible!' said the Supreme Scientist. 'Surely there is *something* we can do!'

'Yes, Your Cognizance, but it will be extremely difficult. The planet is more than five hundred light-years away, and it is very hard to maintain contact. However, we believe we can establish a bridgehead. Unfortunately, that is not the only problem. So far, we have been quite unable to communicate with these beings. Their telepathic powers are exceedingly rudimentary – perhaps even nonexistent. And if we cannot talk to them, there is no way in which we can help.'

There was a long mental silence while the Supreme Scientist analyzed the situation and arrived, as he always did, at the correct answer.

'Any intelligent race must have *some* telepathic individuals,' he mused. 'We must send out hundreds of observers, tuned to catch the first hint of stray thought. When you find a single responsive mind, concentrate all your efforts upon it. We *must* get our message through.'

'Very good, Your Cognizance. It shall be done.'

Across the abyss, across the gulf which light itself took half a thousand years to span, the questing intellects of the planet Thaar sent out their tendrils of thought, searching desperately for a single human being whose mind could perceive their presence. And as luck would have it, they encountered William Cross.

At least, they thought it was luck at the time, though later they were not so sure. In any case, they had little choice. The combination of circumstances that opened Bill's mind to them lasted only for seconds, and was not likely to occur again this side of eternity.

There were three ingredients in the miracle: it is hard to say if one was more important than another. The first was the accident of position. A flask of water, when sunlight falls upon it, can act as a crude lens, concentrating the light into a small area. On an immeasurably larger scale, the dense core of the Earth was converging the waves that came from Thaar. In the ordinary way, the radiations of thought are unaffected by matter – they pass through it as effortlessly as light through glass. But there is rather a lot of matter in a planet, and the whole Earth was acting as a gigantic lens. As it turned, it was carrying Bill through its focus, where the feeble thought impulses from Thaar were concentrated a hundredfold.

Yet millions of other men were equally well placed: they received no message. But they were not rocket engineers: they had not spent years thinking and dreaming of space until it had become part of their very being.

And they were not, as Bill was, blind drunk, teetering on the last knife-edge of consciousness, trying to escape from reality into the world of dreams, where there were no disappointments and setbacks.

Of course, he could see the Army's point of view. 'You are paid, Dr Cross,' General Potter had pointed out with unnecessary emphasis, 'to design missiles, *not* – ah – spaceships. What you do in your spare time is your own concern, but I must ask you not to use the facilities of the establishment for your hobby. From now on, all projects for the computing section will have to be cleared by me. That is all.'

They couldn't sack him, of course: he was too important. But he was not sure that he wanted to stay. He was not really sure of anything except that the job had back-fired on him, and that Brenda had finally gone off with Johnny Gardner – putting events in their order of importance.

Wavering slightly, Bill cupped his chin in his hands and stared at the whitewashed brick wall on the other side of the table. The only attempt at ornamentation was a calendar from Lockheed and a glossy six-by-eight from Aerojet showing L'il Abner Mark I making a boosted take-off. Bill gazed morosely at a spot midway between the two pictures, and emptied his mind of thought. The barriers went down. . . .

At that moment, the massed intellects of Thaar gave a soundless cry of triumph, and the wall in front of Bill slowly dissolved into a swirling mist. He appeared to be looking down a tunnel that stretched to infinity. As a matter of fact, he was.

Bill studied the phenomenon with mild interest. It had a certain novelty, but was not up to the standard of previous hallucinations. And when the voice started to speak in his mind, he let it ramble on for some time before he did anything about it. Even when drunk, he had an old-fashioned prejudice against starting conversations with himself.

'Bill,' the voice began, 'listen carefully. We have had great difficulty in contacting you, and this is extremely important.'

Bill doubted this on general principles. *Nothing* was important any more.

'We are speaking to you from a very distant planet.' continued the voice in a tone of urgent friendliness. 'You are the only human being we have been able to contact, so you *must* understand what we are saying.'

Bill felt mildly worried, though in an impersonal sort of way, since it was now rather hard to focus on his own problems. How serious was it, he wondered, when you started to hear voices? Well, it was best not to get excited. You can take it or leave it, Dr Cross, he told himself. Let's take it until it gets to be a nuisance.

'O.K.,' he answered with bored indifference. 'Go right ahead and talk to me. I won't mind as long as it's interesting.'

There was a pause. Then the voice continued, in a slightly worried fashion.

'We don't quite understand. Our message isn't merely *interesting*. It's vital to your entire race, and you must notify your government immediately.'

'I'm waiting,' said Bill. 'It helps to pass the time.'

Five hundred light-years away, the Thaarns conferred hastily among themselves. Something seemed to be wrong, but they could not decide precisely what. There was no doubt that they had established contact, yet this was not the sort of reaction they had expected. Well, they could only proceed and hope for the best.

'Listen, Bill,' they continued. 'Our scientists have just discovered that your sun is about to explode. It will happen three days from now – seventy-four hours, to be exact. Nothing can stop it. But there's no need to be alarmed. We can save you, if you'll do what we say.'

'Go on,' said Bill. This hallucination was ingenious.

'We can create what we call a bridge – it's a kind of tunnel through space, like the one you're looking into

...w. The theory is far too complicated to explain, even one of your mathematicians.'

'Hold on a minute!' protested Bill. 'I *am* a mathematician, and a darn good one, even when I'm sober. And I've read all about this kind of thing in the science-fiction magazines. I presume you're talking about some kind of short cut through a higher dimension of space. That's old stuff – pre-Einstein.'

A sensation of distinct surprise seeped into Bill's mind. 'We had no idea you were so advanced scientifically,' said the Thaarns. 'But we haven't time to talk about the theory. All that matters is this – if you were to step into that opening in front of you, you'd find yourself instantly on another planet. It's a short cut, as you said – in this case through the thirty-seventh dimension.'

'And it leads to your world?'

'Oh no – you couldn't live here. But there are plenty of planets like Earth in the universe, and we've found one that will suit you. We'll establish bridgeheads like this all over Earth, so your people will only have to walk through them to be saved. Of course, they'll have to start building up civilization again when they reach their new homes, but it's their only hope. You have to pass on this message, and tell them what to do.'

'I can just see them listening to me,' said Bill. 'Why don't you go and talk to the president?'

'Because yours was the only mind we were able to contact. Others seemed closed to us: we don't understand why.'

'I could tell you,' said Bill, looking at the nearly empty bottle in front of him. He was certainly getting his money's worth. What a remarkable thing the human mind was! Of course, there was nothing at all original in this dialogue: it was easy to see where the ideas came from. Only last week he'd been reading a story about the end of the world, and all this wishful thinking about the bridges and tunnels through space was pretty obvious compensation for anyone who'd spent five years wrestling with recalcitrant rockets.

'If the sun does blow up,' Bill asked abruptly – trying to catch his hallucination unawares – 'what would happen?'

'Why, your planet would be melted instantly. All the planets, in fact, right out to Jupiter.'

Bill had to admit that this was quite a grandiose conception. He let his mind play with the thought, and the more he considered it, the more he liked it.

'My dear hallucination,' he remarked pityingly, 'if I believed you, d'you know what I'd say?'

'But you *must* believe us!' came the despairing cry across the light-years.

Bill ignored it. He was warming to his theme.

'I'd tell you this. *It would be the best thing that could possibly happen.* Yes, it would save a whole lot of misery. No one would have to worry about the Russians and the atom bomb and the high cost of living. Oh, it would be wonderful! It's just what everybody really wants. Nice of you to come along and tell us, but just you go back home and pull your old bridge after you.'

There was consternation on Thaar. The Supreme Scientist's brain, floating like a great mass of coral in its tank of nutrient solution, turned slightly yellow about the edges – something it had not done since the Xantil invasion, five thousand years ago. At least fifteen psychologists had nervous breakdowns and were never the same again. The main computer in the College of Cosmophysics started dividing every number in its memory circuits by zero, and promptly blew all its fuses.

And on Earth, Bill Cross was really hitting his stride.

'Look at *me*,' he said, pointing a wavering finger at his chest. 'I've spent years trying to make rockets do something useful, and they tell me I'm only allowed to build guided missiles, so that we can all blow each other up. The sun will make a neater job of it, and if you did give us another planet we'd only start the whole damn thing all over again.'

He paused sadly, marshalling his morbid thoughts.

'And now Brenda heads out of town without even leaving a note. So you'll pardon my lack of enthusiasm for your Boy Scout act.'

He couldn't have said 'enthusiasm' aloud, Bill realized. But he could still think it, which was an interesting scientific discovery. As he got drunker and drunker, would his cogitation – whoops, *that* nearly threw him! – finally drop down to words of one syllable?

In a final despairing exertion, the Thaarns sent their thoughts along the tunnel between the stars.

'You can't really mean it, Bill! Are *all* human beings like you?'

Now that was an interesting philosophical question! Bill considered it carefully – or as carefully as he could in view of the warm, rosy glow that was now beginning to envelop him. After all, things might be worse. He could get another job, if only for the pleasure of telling General Porter what he could do with his three stars. And as for Brenda – well, women were like street-cars: there'd always be another along in a minute.

Best of all, there was a second bottle of whisky in the Top Secret file. Oh, frabjous day! He rose unsteadily to his feet and wavered across the room.

For the last time, Thaar spoke to Earth.

'Bill!' it repeated desperately. 'Surely all human beings can't be like you!'

Bill turned and looked into the swirling tunnel. Strange – it seemed to be lighted with flecks of starlight, and was really rather pretty. He felt proud of himself: not many people could imagine *that*.

'Like me?' he said. 'No, they're not.' He smiled smugly across the light-years, as the rising tide of euphoria lifted him out of his despondency. 'Come to think of it,' he added, 'there are are a lot of people much worse off than me. Yes, I guess I must be one of the lucky ones, after all.'

He blinked in mild surprise, for the tunnel had suddenly collapsed upon itself and the whitewashed wall was there again, exactly as it had always been. Thaar knew it was beaten.

'So much for *that* hallucination,' thought Bill. 'I was getting tired of it, anyway. Let's see what the next one's like.'

As it happened, there wasn't a next one, for five seconds later he passed out cold, just as he was setting the combination of the file cabinet.

The next two days were rather vague and bloodshot, and he forgot all about the interview.

On the third day something was nagging at the back of his mind: he might have remembered if Brenda hadn't turned up again and kept him busy being forgiving.

And there wasn't a fourth day, of course.

A story by Arthur C. Clarke

First Men on the Moon

Astronaut Edwin Aldrin on the surface of the moon, July 1969. The Apollo 11 lunar module is reflected in his faceplate.

Aldrin places the solar wind composition experiment beside the lunar module. The photographs were taken by Neil Armstrong.

THIS IS A TENSE TALE OF THE FUTURE ··· OF THE YEAR 2050, WHEN THINGS WERE PRETTY MUCH AS THEY ARE TODAY, EXCEPT FOR THE CONQUEST OF SPACE. IT'S THE STORY OF A MAN WHO WAS A FAILURE UNTIL HE HITCHED HIS WAGON TO A DISTANT STAR. HE DIDN'T DREAM OF THE PERILS THAT AWAITED HIM WHEN THEY TOLD HIM···

"YOU'LL MAKE a MILLION BUCKS UP THERE!"

STORY: SHANE O'SHEA

ART: CHIC STONE

MEET OUR HERO, **TOM ROBERTSON.** HE DOESN'T SEEM MUCH OF A HERO ··· BUT YOU NEVER CAN TELL···

HOW COME I DON'T SEE YOU IN MY STORE ANYMORE, MRS. GREEN?

LET'S FACE IT··· I MAY DROP IN FOR AN ODD THING OR TWO, BUT WHEN IT COMES TO REAL SHOPPING, YOU JUST CAN'T COMPETE WITH THAT NEW SUPERMARKET!

YES, THAT'S THE WAY THINGS WERE ··· AND SOON···

ROBERTSON'S GROCERY STORE

CLOSED

OUT OF BUSINESS

WHAT GIVES WITH ME ANYWAY, PEGGY? BEFORE THIS, IT WAS THE GENERAL STORE AND I FLOPPED WITH THAT ··· AND BEFORE THAT, IT WAS THE FILLING STATION THAT FOLDED. I··· I GUESS I'M JUST A BORN FAILURE!

NOW, NOW, TOM ··· I LOVE YOU AND I'VE GOT CONFIDENCE IN YOU. SOMEDAY YOU'LL MAKE IT BIG, I'M SURE OF IT!

IT WAS ALL A MATTER OF FINDING THE RIGHT **OPPORTUNITY** ··· AND AN AD IN THE PAPER THE FOLLOWING WEEK SEEMED LIKE JUST THE THING···

MAYBE ··· THIS IS **IT**!

OUT OF THIS WORLD! THAT'S THE CHANCE THAT'S AWAITING YOU IN A GREAT NEW PLANET RECENTLY THROWN OPEN FOR BUSINESS DEVELOPMENT. GREAT OPPORTUNITIES FOR FORWARD LOOKING RETAIL BUSINESSMEN TO MAKE THEIR FORTUNES! APPLY **HARRY Z. GIBBONS**, SUITE 325, ACE BLDG.

YOU LOOK LIKE A SMART BUSINESS-MAN, MR. ROBERTSON. THE PLANET *CORIANTUS* REPRESENTS THE GREATEST COMMERCIAL OPPORTUNITY OF THE AGE! ITS POPULATION NEEDS RETAIL ESTABLISHMENTS --- THEY CAN TAKE EVERYTHING YOU'VE GOT. NOW, IN THE SHOPPING AREA WHICH WE'RE SPONSORING, WE CAN GUARANTEE YOU AN *EXCLUSIVE!*

HERE'S THE GREAT SHOPPING CENTER WE'RE BUILDING AND HERE'S A FINE STORE FOR *YOU.* YOU'LL BE THE ONLY GROCER WITHIN MILES. *YOU'LL MAKE A MILLION BUCKS UP THERE!*

$10,000, YOU SAY? ISN'T THAT A LOT OF MONEY? IT WOULD TAKE EVERY CENT WE COULD BEG OR BORROW ---

BUT LOOK WHAT WE'RE *GETTING* FOR IT, PEG! A FINE STORE, AND THEY'LL TRANSPORT THE STOCK AND US UP THERE FREE. AND LIKE MR. GIBBONS SAYS, I'LL MAKE A MILLION UP THERE! WE *CAN'T* MISS AN OPPORTUNITY LIKE THAT!

FREIGHT ROCKETS TRANSPORTED QUANTITIES OF MERCHANDISE THROUGH SPACE --- AND THERE WAS A PASSENGER CRAFT FOR THE FORWARD-LOOKING BUSINESSMEN AND THEIR FAMILIES ---

ARE *THEY* GOING TO RUN THE OTHER SHOPS IN THE NEW SHOPPING CENTER? I WOULDN'T CALL THEM EXACTLY THE *GO-GETTER* TYPE ---

YOU CAN'T JUDGE BY *LOOKS*, PEG. THEY'RE ALL KEEN OPERATORS WHO KNOW WHAT A REAL OPPORTUNITY IS --- MR. GIBBONS SAYS HE WOULDN'T TAKE ANY OTHER KIND!

IT'S A LONG TRIP. I --- I CAN'T HELP BUT WORRY, TOM. I HOPE IT'S GOING TO BE EVERYTHING YOU SAY ---

HANG IT, PEGGY, STOP WORRYING --- IT'LL BE *FINE!* I WOULDN'T HAVE PAID THE $10,000 IF IT WASN'T A REAL UP-AND-COMING PLACE --- FIRST THING I'LL DO IS JOIN THE ROTARY CLUB --- AND YOU CAN JOIN THE WOMEN'S LITERARY CIRCLE ---

BUT AS THE ROCKET CAME IN FOR A LANDING ON CORIANTUS ---

IS --- IS *THAT* ALL IT IS?

NO TOWN, NO HOUSES, NO PEOPLE --- *NOTHING!*

THE GREAT SHOPPING CENTER WE PAID OUR MONEY FOR --- *LOOK* AT IT!

WE'VE BEEN *CHEATED* --- YOU CAN'T GET AWAY WITH THIS!

LOOK, I DON'T KNOW ANYTHING ABOUT THE WHOLE DEAL. GIBBONS CHARTERED A FLEET OF ROCKETS TO BRING YOU FELLAS AND YOUR STOCKS OF MERCHANDISE UP HERE. YOU GOT ANY COMPLAINTS, TELL 'EM TO *HIM*, NOT US!

THE WORK CREW THAT HAD BUILT THE STORES WAS RETURNING TO EARTH IN THE ROCKET...

YOU'VE BEEN HERE AWHILE, AREN'T THERE...ANY PEOPLE?

OH, SURE, PLENTY OF...PEOPLE! THEY'LL TURN UP, WAIT AND SEE!

ANYWAY, THEY MOVED OUR STOCK INTO THE STORES ...IF ANYBODY EVER COMES TO BUY IT.

SAY, LOOK... WHAT'S THAT SMOKE AND FLAMES COMING FROM THE GROUND?

SHOES

BAKER

MUST BE UNDERGROUND GAS, BURNING. IT HEATS THE GROUND...GUESS THAT'S WHY THEY BUILT THE STORES NEAR IT, FOR THE COLD WEATHER.

UH-HUH...WE MAY STARVE UP HERE, BUT WE WON'T FREEZE!

FOR WANT OF SOMETHING BETTER TO DO, THEY PUT THEIR STOCKS IN ORDER...HOPING FOR CUSTOMERS WHO HADN'T YET APPEARED...

MAYBE WE DID GET CHEATED A LITTLE ON THE STORES... BUT NOT ON THE OPPORTUNITY, AND THAT'S WHAT COUNTS. AFTER ALL, THAT FELLA SAID THERE'S PLENTY OF PEOPLE AND THEY'LL TURN UP!

YES, BUT WHERE ARE THEY...?

SHE DIDN'T KNOW IT, BUT HER QUESTION WAS BEING ANSWERED AT THAT VERY MOMENT...

GROCERY

TOM... L-LOOK...

STEADY, PEG...THEY'RE MUTANTS! THERE MUST HAVE BEEN A RADIO-ACTIVE WAR UP HERE AGES AGO THAT CHANGED THE FUTURE GENERATIONS. BUT THAT DOESN'T MEAN THEY WON'T BE GOOD CUSTOMERS...

GOOD CUSTOMERS? THEY DIDN'T ACT LIKE IT...

HOLD ON...YOU CAN'T DO THAT! I'M SUPPOSED TO WAIT ON YOU AND THEN YOU PAY ME FOR WHATEVER YOU WANT...

3

WE'LL DO WHATEVER WE WANT, EARTHLING!

POW

THE MUTANTS SPOKE THE INTERPLANETARY COMMON LANGUAGE... WHEN WE'VE FINISHED WITH WHAT WE'VE TAKEN... WE'LL BE BACK FOR MORE!

CAME AT ME... DIDN'T GIVE ME A CHANCE...

YOU DIDN'T HAVE A CHANCE FROM THE BEGINNING. GIBBONS TOOK YOU FOR YOUR $10,000... AND NOW THOSE SAVAGES ARE TAKING YOU FOR THE LAST THING YOU OWN... YOUR STOCK. YOU'RE JUST A SUCKER, TOM ROBERTSON... A SHEEP!

YOU CAN'T TALK TO ME LIKE THAT! YOU MAKE ME SOUND LIKE... LIKE A FOOL!

WHAT ELSE DO YOU THINK YOU ARE? EVER SINCE I MARRIED YOU, YOU'VE BEEN A FAILURE, A COWARD, A NE'ERDOWELL. AND NOW YOU'VE HIT THE BOTTOM!

OH, GOD, FORGIVE ME FOR THE WAY I SPOKE TO HIM... BUT IF EVER THERE WAS A TIME WHEN HE HAD TO FIGHT, IT'S NOW! WILL HE DO IT... OR CRY ABOUT HIS LOSSES AND FAIL AGAIN?

I'VE LOST EVERYTHING... MONEY, DREAMS, EVEN PEG'S LOVE. SHE SAID I WAS A FAILURE, A COWARD, AND SHE'S RIGHT...

NO... SHE'S WRONG! SHE EXPECTS ME TO FOLD UP... WELL ... WE'LL SEE ABOUT THAT!

HE FOUND THE OTHER SHOPKEEPERS DISTRAUGHT, DEFEATED BY THE CRUEL RAID...

IF ONLY WE COULD TAKE OUR LOSSES AND GO BACK... BUT HOW? THERE'S NO ROCKET TO TAKE US...

AND THOSE MUTANTS WILL ATTACK TIME AFTER TIME, TILL THEY TAKE THE LAST THING WE'VE GOT... AND WE'LL STARVE UP HERE!

WAIT A SECOND, YOU GUYS! I'VE GOT SOMETHING TO SAY TO YOU!

4

5

THERE'S A COUPLE OF 'EM APPROACHING WITH A WHITE FLAG, ROBERTSON. LOOKS AS IF THEY WANT TO CONFER...

WHITE FLAG, EH? OKAY...CAN'T BE ANY HARM IN GOING OUT AND TALKING TO THEM.

BUT NO SOONER HAD HE ADVANCED TO THE FLAG OF TRUCE WHEN...

THEY WON'T DARE TURN LOOSE ANYMORE OF THOSE ROCKS FOR FEAR OF INJURING HIM! QUICK...LET'S GRAB HIM AND HEAD FOR THE TREES!

COK!

TOM ROBERTSON CAME TO IN THE MUTANT VILLAGE...

WHAT A FOOL I WAS...TO TRUST YOU! WHY DIDN'T YOU FINISH ME OFF RIGHT AWAY...WHY DID YOU BRING ME HERE?

ONLY BECAUSE WE WANTED TO FIND OUT WHAT OTHER WEAPONS YOU MIGHT HAVE TO USE AGAINST US.

THEY HAD THEIR WAYS OF EXTRACTING INFORMATION...

I'M TELLING YOU...WE HAVE NO ARMS...NO WEAPONS...JUST...THOSE CATAPULTS...

I THINK HE'S TELLING THE TRUTH!

WELL, THE REST OF YOUR KIND WILL DISCOVER THAT CATAPULTS ARE USELESS AGAINST THEM! WHEN WE STRIKE AGAIN, IT WILL BE IN FORCE, RIDING THOSE CREATURES...AND THERE WON'T BE A SINGLE ONE OF YOU LEFT!

AND I SUPPOSE YOU'RE GOING TO START OFF BY HAVING ME EXECUTED, RIGHT?

RIGHT...AND WE PLAN TO ENJOY THE PROCEEDINGS. YOU SEE, YOU'RE GOING TO GET A CLOSER LOOK AT ONE OF OUR PETS ...ONE THAT HASN'T BEEN TAMED YET!

GUESS I'M ...UP AGAINST IT...

GARRR-RRR...

···WELL··HERE COMES THE LAST ACT FOR A *FAILURE!* THIS IS THE ONLY THING I CAN USE··BUT AT LEAST I'LL GO OUT *FIGHTING!*

RRR-RRRR···

EEE-YOWWWW!

EEEE-EEEeeeeee!

WANT *OUT,* DO YOU? WELL, I'M COMING ALONG!

CRASH!

THAT'S HOW TOM WAS ABLE TO BRING BACK NEWS OF THE FRIGHTFUL ATTACK WHICH LOOMED···

DINOSAURS! WE'RE THROUGH, THEN··· OUR CATAPULTS AND THE WALL COULD NEVER HOLD OFF A CHARGE LIKE THAT!

THEY SURE COULDN'T···BUT I'VE GOT A BRAIN-STORM WHICH JUST MIGHT BE THE ANSWER···

GROCER

···AND THERE IT IS! WE'VE GOT OUR WORK CUT OUT FOR US, BUT OLD MOTHER NATURE'S GOING TO HELP. WE'RE GOING TO TAP SOME OF THAT UNDERGROUND GAS, AND WE'VE GOT TO BUILD THE PROPER APPARATUS TO USE IT!

THE DEFENDERS WORKED FEVERISHLY AGAINST TIME TO CONSTRUCT WHAT HE WANTED···

STEP IT UP···THEY MAY ATTACK ANY MINUTE NOW, AND OUR ONLY CHANCE IS TO HAVE THIS STUFF *READY!*

7

ANOTHER WHITE FLAG, CHIEF! PROBABLY TREACHERY AGAIN

I DON'T THINK SO... I'M BETTING THEY KNOW WHEN THEY'RE LICKED. HAVE THE DELEGATION ADVANCE INTO HERE... BUT STAY ON GUARD!

WE'RE SURRENDERING OUR LEADER TO YOU... ALL THIS WAS HIS FAULT. SPARE US, WE BEG OF YOU... WE KNOW WE CAN'T FIGHT YOU...

THERE'S NO NEED FOR FIGHTING... ACTUALLY WE CAN GET ALONG VERY WELL TOGETHER. WE HAVE THINGS TO SELL... THINGS THAT YOU NEED.

PSSST... CHIEF...

HOW CAN WE SELL THEM ANYTHING? THEY HAVE NO MONEY...

MAYBE NOT... BUT HAVE YOU NOTICED THE ORNAMENTS THEY WEAR? I'M BETTING THEY'LL TEST AS SOLID GOLD... AND THAT THEY'LL GLADLY TRADE 'EM FOR WHATEVER WE'RE WILLING TO SWAP!

SOME TIME HAD PASSED WHEN PROMOTER HARRY Z. GIBBONS RECEIVED AN UNEXPECTED VISITOR DOWN ON PLANET EARTH...

T-TOM ROBERTSON! HOW... W-WHAT...

SO YOU REMEMBER ME, DO YOU... AND YOU'RE PROBABLY WONDERING HOW I EVER GOT BACK FROM CORIANTUS.

WELL, IT SO HAPPENED THAT A GEOPHYSICAL EXPLORATION ROCKET LANDED, AND WE WERE ABLE TO ARRANGE FOR REGULAR SERVICE BETWEEN CORIANTUS AND EARTH.

BUT... BUT WHAT DID YOU WANT THE SERVICE FOR? WHO'D WANT TO GO THERE? COME BACK, YES ...BUT GO...?

WHAT A QUESTION TO ASK... DIDN'T YOU TELL ME I'D MAKE A MILLION BUCKS UP THERE? WELL, I DID... I JUST THOUGHT YOU'D LIKE TO KNOW!

THANKS... THANKS A MILLION!... WELL, WHAT DO YOU KNOW... HE FAINTED!

THE END!

9

The Andromeda Nebula

The Andromeda Nebula, a galaxy which contains perhaps 200,000,000,000 stars, is 2,300,000 light years from us, so this photograph shows it as it looked 2,300,000 years ago. The Milky Way galaxy, on the rim of which is our solar system, probably resembles it in appearance. Astronomers believe the number of galaxies in the parts of the universe that we can at present observe may be as high as 100,000,000,000.

Photograph from the Mount Wilson and Palomar Observatories.

Space Travel

One day – it may be in this century, or it may be a thousand years from now – we shall discover a really efficient means of propelling our space-vehicles. The ultimate speed for spaceships is the velocity of light. They will never reach that goal, but they will get very close to it. And then the nearest star will be less than five years' voyaging from Earth.

Our exploring ships will spread outwards from their home over an ever-expanding sphere of space. It is a sphere which will grow at almost – but never quite – the speed of light. Even voyages which may last for centuries or millennia will one day be attempted.

Looking far into the future we must picture a slow (little more than half a billion miles an hour!) expansion of human activities outwards from the Solar System, among the suns scattered across the region of the galaxy in which we now find ourselves. These suns are on the average five light-years apart; in other words, we can never get from one to the next in less than five years.

At this point we will deal with an obvious objection. Can we be *sure* that the velocity of light is indeed a limiting factor? So many 'impassable' barriers have been shattered in the past; perhaps this one may go the way of all the others.

Scientists believe that light can never be outraced by any form of radiation or any material object. Let us assume the contrary and see just where it gets us. We will even take the most optimistic possible case, and imagine that the speed of transportation may eventually become infinite.

Picture a time when, by the development of techniques as far beyond our present engineering as a transistor is beyond a stone axe, we can reach anywhere we please *instantaneously,* with no more effort than by dialling a number. This would indeed cut the Universe down to size, and reduce its physical immensity to nothingness. What would be left?

Everything that really matters. For the Universe has two aspects – its scale, and its overwhelming, mind-numbing complexity. Having abolished the first, we are now face-to-face with the second.

What we must now try to visualize is not size, but quantity. Most people today are familiar with the simple notation which scientists use to describe large numbers; it consists merely of counting zeros, so that a hundred becomes 10^2, a million, 10^6; a billion, 10^9 and so on.

The number of other suns in our own galaxy is estimated at about 10^{11} – or written in full, 100,000,000,000. Our present telescopes can observe something like 10^9 other galaxies, and they show no sign of thinning out even at the extreme limit of vision. There are probably at least as many galaxies in the whole of creation as there are stars in our own galaxy, but let us confine ourselves to those we can see. They must contain a total of about 10^{11} times 10^9 stars, or 10^{20} stars altogether.

1 followed by 20 other digits is, of course, a number beyond understanding. There is no hope of ever coming to grips with it, but there are ways of hinting at its implications.

Just now we assumed that the time might come when we could move ourselves, by some miracle of matter-transmission, effortlessly and instantly round the Cosmos, as today we call a number in our local exchange. What would the Cosmic Telephone Direstory look like, if its contents were restricted to suns and it made no effort to list individual planets, still less the millions of places on each planet?

The directories for such cities as London and New York are already getting somewhat out of hand, but they list only about a million – 10^6 – numbers. The Cosmic Directory would be 10^{14} times bigger, to hold its 10^{20} numbers.

To continue our fantasy a little further, here is another consequence of 20-digit telephone numbers. Think of the possibilities of cosmic chaos, if dialling 27945015423811986385 instead of 27945015243811986385 could put you at the wrong end of Creation. . . . This is no trifling example; look well and carefully at these arrays of digits, savouring their weight and meaning, remembering that we may need every one of them to count the total tally of the stars, and even more to number their planets.

Before such numbers, even spirits brave enough to face the challenge of the light-years must quail. The detailed examination of all the grains of sand on all the beaches of the world is a far smaller task than the exploration of the universe.

From *Profiles of the Future*
by Arthur C. Clarke

✸ starscope ✸

CAPRICORN (Dec. 22-Jan. 20)

Saturn, now settled where it concerns your love-life, has fine aspects from the Sun and Venus. These give you greater assurance and confidence that what you have in love is strong and lasting, and leaves you free to ponder on plans connected with work or home. In this area you are not quite certain just what you want, and only time will tell. If you are doing any sort of writing on the 18th, the outcome will be terrifically successful. Towards the end of the month you have a sudden unexpected meeting with a friend, which delights you.

AQUARIUS (Jan. 21-Feb. 19)

An interplay between Mercury and Venus on the 7th suggests that you'll be discussing an enterprise with someone you're very fond of. If the time is ripe, this could be marriage. Quite a little bagful of money should turn up on the 25th or round about that time. You go through your old clothes and team them up with new ones to make a fascinating wardrobe. Many Aquarian Honeys will consider changing their career as unexpected possibilities and help are offered. Use all your enterprise. A disappointment in a letter—forget it. Some gay get-togethers.

PISCES (Feb. 20-March 20)

Your career should be in the forefront of your mind this month; perhaps you should extend your activities, instead of resting on your oars. However, this will be difficult for you because Venus and Neptune are discordant just now, and cause you to have wild romantic longings and fancies, not all of which will materialise. Pisceans starting a later holiday are promised a marvellous time; others may have a well-aspected weekend trip that takes them to the clouds. There is one extraordinary occurrence this month, to mystify you, which ends in laughter.

ARIES (March 21-April 20)

When Mercury joins Uranus late this month, you may get confused—possibly through held-up communications—about someone's marriage, and thus cause offence. Straighten out your diary and watch put. This is a month when you're going to go in for a new image in a big way. You'll change your hairstyle and probably colour, get some smashing new clothes and have a quite new slant on life. You'll impress where you want to, and you'll be amazed at the helpful friendliness that surrounds you. New friends of the type you want to meet come along.

TAURUS (April 21-May 21)

Much of your life lately has been centred round your home, but on the 22nd Venus' amiable influence moves to life and love, so plan your activities accordingly. Life jets along at the end of the month. There is news of an old boyfriend and a pleasant interlude, but it doesn't 'take' this time and there are no regrets. A tough job of work is put your way, but you see it through firmly. An opportunity to eat more rich foods than usual and, being a Taurean, you'll take it. Keep an eye on that streamline. Watch what you say on the 13th —you'll encounter a touchy person.

GEMINI (May 22-June 21)

Mercury joins Jupiter on the 4th and again on the 22nd. Both these days are successful if you are in a money-raising group, bringing fun as well as funds. There is some sort of show-down in the middle of the month—you simply have to know where you are. A very important letter arrives about the 13th and further news on the 23rd, posing a choice. As you don't want to make one, you remain as you are, sitting on the fence. Don't be rushed into anything you don't want to do. You are not mistaken about someone's odd attitude, but you've been misjudged.

CANCER (June 22-July 22)

After the solar eclipse on the 11th, you suddenly change your mind about something you have been aiming at. You watch someone else's progress and decide to do something quite different, but the energy you've already spent on an ambition won't be wasted. All partnerships are under good signs. The first and last days of the month are specially important and a happy pact is made. Your lucky number is 2 and you should use this wherever possible. You'll be upset by a remark from a thoughtless friend, but don't be on the defensive; keep cheerful.

LEO (July 23-Aug. 23)

When Mercury joins the Sun this month you will revise your ideas about one or two men you know. It might be your boss, and boyfriend or husband. In any case, it leads to a better understanding all round. Don't be secretive about your change of ideas, though. You take on an extra activity for which you really haven't time and meet some very interesting people, with similar outlook. Something you read you identify with yourself and this gives you a new slant on future plans. You come to one crossroads—take bold action.

VIRGO (Aug. 24-Sept. 23)

The New Moon in your sign on the 11th brings changes affecting your job or domestic affairs, more likely the former. You are not sure at the time if you like these or not, even if you have brought them about yourself. Mark time before plunging into even another fresh project. Something that is just your cup of tea is going to come along and you don't want to be too tied up. The last week brings an intensely happy romantic episode which scatters some already-made plans to the wind. The 18th is a day to watch for straws showing which way the wind is blowing.

LIBRA (Sept. 24-Oct. 23)

Venus' link with Jupiter on the 5th indicates that a good friend will put you in the way of making some extra cash. Also, there is an introduction to someone rather highly-placed socially. In fact, there is a lot of help and real luck to do with both business and love. On a journey on the 22nd you will be given some very good advice, but will fight against taking it. Something that you put in motion a year or two ago should come back into your plans again and pay off handsomely. Blue soothes and is lucky this month for all Librans.

SCORPIO (Oct. 24-Nov. 22)

Neptune, now in your sign, is angled by the Sun on the 19th. If you are taking a late holiday by water, you may be surprised to find that something good connected with your career happens then. You will have a lot to do with a Club or society and will win laurels for your helpful work. Your spare time will be taken right up. It'll be an expensive month and, if you are a married Honey, your household budget may strain at the seams. Where a contract is concerned, read it very carefully and make sure it is just as you want it.

SAGITTARIUS (Nov. 23-Dec. 21)

Although throughout the month your social life is hectic, the Full Moon on the 25th temporarily damps it down. Before that, the 3rd, 9th and 13th bring happy parties. You should be flush money-wise, and on the 8th go out and do some luxury shopping, buying several things you had thought were out of your reach. You'll be in the limelight mainly through boyfriend or husband. However, your love-life takes some handling and don't confide in too many people or you'll get conflicting advice. You are unsure and rocked about on waves of emotion.

From *Honey*

Horoscopes

Forecast for Gemini on the 28th of March this year.

Daily Express 'Good day for any kind of desk work'.

Sun 'An action-packed phase'.

Daily Mirror 'You can relax'.

Daily Mail 'This will be an unusual day'.

Most people will say there's nothing in horoscopes. So you would expect that most people wouldn't read them. But they do.

We thought we would try to find out how useful forecasts from stars really are, in their most accessible form – horoscopes in the press.

In this report the ones we are looking at are those in the daily and Sunday newspapers, and the women's magazines, which are by far the most widely read. We looked in particular at the four magazines or newspapers in each class with the widest circulation – the *Daily Express, Daily Mail, Daily Mirror,* and *Sun;* the *Sunday Mirror, Sunday Express, People* and *News of the World;* and *Woman's Own, Woman, Woman's Realm* and *Woman's Weekly.*

Do people use horoscopes?

First of all we asked 1,000 people whether they read horoscopes, whether they found them useful, and what their reactions were.

Their reactions ranged from nonsense' and 'a load of rubbish' through 'they're fun' and 'amusing', to one person who always looked at them 'before making any major decision'.

Some people had mixed feelings about the qualifications of newspaper horoscope writers in general. 'Somebody told me that they're not really experts, they just write what comes into their heads', was one comment. A second person was more certain – 'horoscopes are written by amateurs'. But a third was much more sympathetic – 'they only do it for a living' was her comment. Finally one woman confided, 'If *The Times* had one, I'd change to it.'

But, whatever they said, most people – eight out of ten men, and seven out of ten women – were convinced that horoscopes were not of any practical use.

In spite of this, we found that more than eight out of ten – both men and women – do still read them, at least occasionally, and about half of these read them fairly regularly. The thought of reading something about ourselves must be too much for our curiosity – 'I'm disillusioned, but I still read them', said one person we interviewed.

To find out how good the advice and predictions really are, and see if there was any best buy, we asked some 200 people, some men, some women, some believers and some not, to read their horoscopes in the papers and magazines every day for a month, and to comment on them at the end of each day.

Were the horoscopes helpful?

When the future is so baffling that you resort to reading horoscopes, you will probably be hoping to get some more significant advice than you could get from a friend. For example, you don't just want to be told, on the day after the Budget, to 'give extra time to financial matters'.

So first of all we asked our horoscope readers to

say whether they found the advice at all helpful, irrespective of whether it was accurate or not.

Rather sadly, 83 per cent reported that the advice was very little help at all. There wasn't much to choose between any of the newspapers and magazines we looked at but *Woman*, *Woman's Own* and the *Daily Mirror* were thought marginally less unhelpful than the average, while the *Sun* and the *News of the World* were thought worse.

Were the horoscopes accurate?

Even if they are not very helpful, horoscopes might at least be quite accurate. So we then asked our readers to say whether any predicted events actually happened.

Even worse: this time 87 per cent reported that predictions were not really very accurate at all.

Three magazines, *Woman*, *Woman's Own* and *Woman's Weekly*, were thought slightly less disastrously inaccurate than average, while the *Sunday Mirror* and once again the *Sun* and the *News of the World* were thought to be worse.

How important is your sign?

Before you read your horoscope you have to decide what sign you were born under. Unfortunately you may find that this depends on what newspaper you happen to be reading, as they could never all agree when one sign ended and the other began. The women's magazines, for example, could not even agree on the dates of Virgo. *Woman* and *Woman's Realm* thought it was from August 22 to September 22, *Woman's Own* from August 23 to September 22, and *Woman's Weekly* from August 24 to September 23. In fact, the dates of the signs change slightly from year to year. If you were born at the beginning or end of a sign, you'll have to go back to the records of the year you were born, and know the exact hour of your birth, to be sure which sign you do come under.

Having gone to the trouble to discover your sign, just how significant is it? We checked this by sending predictions from the horoscopes to our helpers, and asking them how accurate they were. What we didn't tell them was that some of the predictions were for their own sign, and some were for completely different ones. Of course, if there was anything in them, predictions for their own sign should have been conspicuously more accurate.

Unfortunately the results proved otherwise. There was absolutely no difference in accuracy between reading your own horoscope and reading any other one.

Men v Women

Many men immediately seem to associate a belief in horoscopes with gullible women. The famous twelfth century Jewish physician, Moses Maimonides wrote: 'Anyone who has faith in these and similar things, and believes in his heart that they contain truth and wisdom . . . belongs to the fools and the senseless, and is to be classed with women and children.'

Some of the men we interviewed were pretty scathing too. 'Only put in for women.' 'Only naïve women read them' and 'Ridiculous nonsense, but it's to attract the female element isn't it?' were some of the comments they made. One felt positively protective about this, 'misleading to little girls' he said.

So we thought we would check to see whether men were more critical of horoscopes than women.

We did find that about 5 per cent more women than men found the advice useful, and the predictions accurate. On the other hand, our survey actually showed that more men than women were ready to believe that it was possible to tell the future – five out of ten as opposed to four out of ten.

And, as we have already seen, almost exactly the same proportion of men as of women actually read the horoscopes. So it's clear that, when it comes to horoscopes, there's not as much difference between the sexes as some men would like to think.

Conclusions

In this report we have looked at the most popular horoscopes in the press. Even professional astrologers would probably tell you that they are ·too general to be of any use, and would not consider them true horoscopes.

The vast ·majority of people who checked their horoscopes for us systematically found that the advice was useless and the predictions inaccurate.

But our survey suggests that, on present form, most of us will still go on reading them.

So is there a Best Buy?

We have found that there is no difference in accuracy between predictions whichever sign you read. So, if you want to cheer yourself up, the best thing to do is to read all the predictions and pick out the one you like best. It's no more likely to be inaccurate than any of the others.

A report in *Which?*

The Witch Doctor

Different people have different superstitions. This Zulu witch doctor is invoking rain during a time of drought. If he is unsuccessful, he will explain that the fault is not his. It must be because some ritual detail in the preparatory ceremonies has been omitted by one of the villagers.

Your Sunday Paper

The paper with the largest circulation in the world – it claims to be the 'greatest' in all ways – is the *News of the World*. It is certainly the most notorious, so that everyone knows what is meant when a character in a famous modern play warns his friend that he will end up in the *News of the World*.

Sex stories are more regularly and fully reported in this paper than in any other. They tend to be stories which most other papers disregard as too obvious or trivial. Certainly, such stories as 'Wife and the Man Next Door', or 'Loving Glances for the Lodger' sound like items from any local gossip's agenda, and for a regular reader there must be a certain monotony in these stories, only alleviated by items like 'Death Takes a Hand at Strip Poker', or 'Vicar Chased Me over Pews, says Choirboy'.

The most obscure events can make the pages of the *News of the World* if they are, or can be made to appear, titillating. 'Two Wives Plan by Court Clerk' makes a double-column story on the front page. It turns out to be a report of a talk to an obscure gathering in which the speaker, a court clerk, speculated on the possible advantages of duogamy. Similar circumstances in which the speaker advanced unusual views about industry or war would be unlikely to be noticed by the paper. There is a certain irony in one story which describes a 'sordid magazine' whose contents, style and ownership the paper fearlessly exposes.

The *News of the World* has a high proportion of readers who are working-class and no longer very young. Women readers of all ages are presumably expected to identify themselves with the reported experience of a French girl of seventeen who is marrying a millionaire of thirty-one. She had achieved, said the caption, something that many a girl has dreamed of. Many more women readers would be able to identify with the long story of the misfortunes of a lady, photographed in scarf and curlers, who won £100 at bingo and then found her prize withheld because of a technicality. And perhaps many men will find in another story something *they* have often dreamed of. It deals with a man who won a huge sum on the pools, and now devotes his life wholly to searching for 'Miss Wonderful' – a search which has led him on long journeys and to innumerable hotel rooms with contenders for the title. Such a life,

combining lots of money and non-stop amorous adventures, might be taken as a goal for living by many readers. After all, Don Juan was a character of fiction; this man is real.

A regular competition, usually involving judgements about clothes, pays handsome prizes; and a special one invites wives to enter their milkman for the Personality Milkman Competition, in which they could win £100 for themselves, and a similar amount for their milkman. Remembering working-class lore about the relations between housewives and their milkmen (neglected by Hoggart in *The Uses of Literacy*, but see that other authority, Ken Dodd) this seems an ingenious competition, and one which fits the general ethos of the paper.

There are other things in the paper, of course – it gives more political news than some of its rivals; but the general atmosphere is that of Coronation Street plus the viciousness of that world which the television programme omits. Prostitution rears its ugly head in these columns, and so does murder.

The world of the *News of the World* is a slightly old-fashioned one, though it has changed somewhat in the past few years. It is still a long way from the 'swinging' style of the *Sunday Mirror*.

Here serious news takes up relatively little space, though it often dominates the front page. A tit-bit about a small-town headmaster who forbids his pupils to see a performance of Brecht's *Caucasian Chalk Circle* because of the 'rude words' in it, makes a large top-of-the-page headline, completely dwarfing an attack on the Government by the Leader of the Opposition. Pop stars are frequently pictured and reported, most of a page being given to an account of a singer's nerves before a performance, and how she copes with them. Since pop stars are idols for many young people, such an article may be helpful in showing them that their heroes get nerves like the rest of us.

Pin-up pictures are regular features. These, too, offer sexy styles for women readers to imitate, and for men to cherish as their image of 'Miss Wonderful'. It is going too far to say, as some moralists do, that such pictures are corrupting; but they are certainly misleading. They mislead us about the nature of woman and her role. You can't imagine a pin-up changing a baby's nappy or washing the dishes, and if that seems an old-fashioned view of woman's role, it would be equally difficult to envisage a pin-up running a school or a business. Pin-up pictures also encourage a cattle-market approach to women, an approach echoed in the following caption to one picture: 'A beautiful girl who lacks vivacity is like a boiled egg without salt. A plain girl with too much of it is like a live herring on a fishmonger's slab. Vivacity must be attuned to the goods on offer'.

' . . . *The goods on offer*' is a blatantly give-away phrase to use about a woman. No wonder the same caption begins by saying that 'The Mona Lisa has her admirers, but few people would choose her as the ideal companion for a night out on the tiles.'

The *Daily Mirror* developed during the war a tradition of representing everyman's grouses against authority. The tradition is carried on in the *Sunday Mirror* where there is a regular column called 'Ombudsmirror'. It reports readers' experiences of the complex obtuseness of the Inland Revenue, or the petty tyrannies of Local Government. On the opposite page, a columnist who acts as the 'Sunday Mirror Weekend Girl', describes the frustrations of trying to get delivery of Coalite from a large London distributor. (Almost all the Sundays have begun to represent consumer interests much more than they did before the rise of the Consumer Movement and journals like *Which*.) I counted nine named columnists in one issue of the *Sunday Mirror*, excluding film, television, and sports writers. One reviews politics; another advises on value for money in shopping; others dispense legal and medical advice. Columnist Anne Allen is described as 'the writer who gets to the heart of things'. Typical of her approach is the headline: LET'S HAVE A STANDARD FOR HUMAN KINDNESS. The article beneath challenges the comfortable to be aware of the plight of the disabled, and argues that not enough is spent on services for the disabled. 'Our priorities are cock-eyed if we spend millions on weapons that will soon be obsolete and let suffering on this scale continue for the lack of a little hard cash.

'What *does* matter? Military honours or the milk of human kindness? You tell me.'

Miss Allen symbolises one aspect of the *Mirror* – its earthy common sense and human compassion, tinged with sentimentality. These are the qualities which lead it to devote a centre-page spread to a striking picture of the men and equipment needed to rescue one pot-holer in difficulties. It eloquently makes the point that here is an inordinate expenditure of money and human resources.

The *Sunday Mirror* is not so much a newspaper, as a parish magazine for a large part of the population of Britain. It really seeks to serve its readers – though at the same time pandering to them. It speaks to and for the well-heeled working-class reader, offering him some sort of guide through the complexities of modern living. It is more concerned with general problems than with the narrower aspects of style exemplified in features on food and clothing.

A similar warm humanism (like the fug in a working-class pub on a Saturday night) pervades the *People*. 'Man O' the People' addresses his readers as 'My friends', and solicits their support for good causes. Even a report on Vietnam opens with a direct personal approach: 'Have you ever felt unloved and unwanted, hated in fact?' Common decency is championed in the condemnation of a wrestling bout between a man and a woman; and in a coyly blanked-out photo report about a topless waitress, the caption takes a conventional line: 'Sorry, madam, we prefer you properly dressed'. However, the *People* tries to have its cake and eat it. It front-pages a picture of a slim actress in a bath towel ('You've never seen Hayley like THIS before!') to introduce the serialised version of a film about an unconsummated marriage. It devotes a whole page to a *News of the World*-type story of a ' "girl" secretary who is a married man'. It piously endorses the Press Council's declaration that no payment should be made to 'persons engaged in crime or other notorious misbehaviour', but two weeks later serialises the personal story of the wife of a train robber, who lived with him while he was on the run. ('I don't regret what I did – standing by my husband, whatever he had done.') It even uses the old *Reveille* trick of the shocking headline for an innocuous story: HAPPINESS IS TWO WIVES, is in fact the story of a writer-husband who is 'married' to his typewriter. Still, the paper does oppose a major trend in the sixties style in Britain with articles on compulsive gambling, which depict it as a disease needing medical and psychiatric treatment. It also features sensible advice from a married woman magistrate on how parents should handle the emotional problems of their sons and daughters. To use its own language, the *People* 'leads an astonishing double life', and perhaps encourages its readers to double think in their own lives.

From an article by Roy Shaw in
Your Sunday Paper, edited by Richard Hoggart

Nuts to the Neophili cs!

▲ AN UGLY word has come into the English language. NEOPHILIAC. And it has an ugly meaning.

A neophiliac is anyone who suffers from a dangerous disease—falling in love with everything that is new.

The disease has been raging throughout the fifties and sixties, according to the man who invented the word, Mr. Christopher Booker.

In The Neophiliacs (Collins, 42s.) he describes the symptoms of the illness and names many of the prominent people who have succumbed to it.

From the earnest bishop who defended Lady Chatterley's Lover for its portrayal of sex as "an act of holy communion," to the distinguished critic who hailed the Beatles as "the greatest composers since Beethoven."

There's nothing new about sex (of course), or about the rise of a highly talented group. Fair enough to welcome the new, and healthier frankness about sex, and the new, and exciting, sounds of the latest pop.

What is **DOTTY** and **DEPLORABLE** is the extravagant adoration that is given to the latest fad, fashion or fancy in manners and morals by people who should know better.

DOTTY, because it just isn't true that "new" automatically equals "good." It is often bad.

DEPLORABLE, because embracing

VOICE OF The People

the new often means throwing over old values that are good, and giving great offence to millions who cling to them.

Remember, for example, the shock of outrage when Kenneth Tynan used that four-letter word on the B.B.C.

We won't print the word, even though by doing so we would win the acclaim of the sophisticates (in future we'll have to call them the neophiliacs).

We won't print it because, though it does not worry us or many of our readers in the least, its use is deeply hurtful to those brought up with a horror of four-letter crudities.

The neophiliacs have no regard for the feelings of these people. They trample not only old traditions, but on those who cherish them.

Only for the young and their youthful crazes do the neophiliacs show real sympathy. They applaud the revolutionary current started by our bright university sparks. (It must be good; it's new!)

And the whole country is bamboozled into believing that top priority has to be given to students' grievances.

Last week a Select Committee of the House of Commons produced, in record time, a report urging radical reforms in higher education.

Good for the students, perhaps. But what about the **real** national priority the **really** underprivileged—the slum-dwellers, the homeless, the aged, the mentally sick?

They go to the back of the queue Investigating and remedying their plight is not so urgent, it seems, a dealing with the problems of the new and pushful student generation.

Caring for the genuine underdog one of those old values that is being displaced by the mania for new ones

That's a measure of the damage done by the neophiliacs in the fifties and sixties.

Theirs is a disease that must be cured if Britain in the seventies is to become a more decent and not a more demented society.

We prefer a better word than neophiliac. That word is CRUSADER

A CRUSADER FIGHTS TO MAKE THE WORLD A BETTER PLACE. AND WELCOMES THE NEW — IF IT'S GOOD.

From *The People*

SOME TYPICAL GIRLS TELL...

How I became a prostitute

A PRETTY, 20-year-old brunette wearing jeans and carrying an overnight bag, arrived at King's Cross Station and took her first wide-eyed look at London a few months ago.

Today her parents in Leeds think that their daughter is earning a good living as a model.

The weekly sums of money they receive from her are to them proof of her success. In fact, Jean earns her living picking up men in Soho. She waits for clients emerging from the X-film cinemas and takes them to one of several obliging hotels in Bayswater.

What happened to Jean after her arrival in London? How did she get "on the game"?

Her story is similar to

BY KEN GARDNER
and a team of People reporters

that of scores of girls who come to London every year.

But the reasons *why* and *how* these girls become prostitutes are quite diverse and provide psychologists with no set pattern.

Money, as must be expected, is a big reason—but these girls are often from middle and upper class families.

But let us take the case of Jean, who left Leeds after a row with her parents—who are separated—and her boy-friend.

She came to London determined, with her flair for clothes and her good looks, to get a job in the fashion business.

She knew nobody in the capital and had nowhere to stay. From the moment she arrived she was lonely She spent the first night crying in the bed-sitter she found for herself at Highgate.

The next day, while having a cup of coffee in a snack-bar, she found a pleasant young man sitting next to her, who seemed as lonely as herself.

He introduced himself as Eric.

They had a long chat and, as she herself admits, " I was hating the moment to arrive when I knew he would have to go."

But that moment came and the young man got up from the table and said he had a date but would like to see her in the same place the following day.

She did meet him again and by the end of the week they were close friends. He took her to discotheques and Soho drinking-clubs and she was flattered because he had chosen her to show around.

When he invited her to move in with him at his flat in Balham, in South London, she did not hesitate.

She still had not found a job, but she had a few pounds left. In any case, her boy-friend was not short of money.

About a month after they met, however, he told her that he had lost all his money playing cards. He was heavily in debt to a friend and needed money quickly.

As he was explaining this, there was a knock on the door and the friend came into the room. There were a few sharp words with Eric, who suddenly left the room and left Jean with the friend.

Of course, it was just a plot between the two men. After an hour or so the friend had persuaded the girl to sleep with him in exchange for settling her boy-friend's debt.

It was not long before Eric pretended to need money again, and he did not have a great deal of trouble in persuading his girl-friend to help him.

" I thought I was in love with him," she told People investigators. " In the end I was sleeping with all his friends for money. He took every penny.

" I realised then that he had only been using me. But it was such an easy way to make money that I left him and carried on doing it alone.

" Then I met another fellow and I am living with him. He knows I am on the game, but we don't talk about it."

Jean starts work soon after midday and reckons to reach home by 8 p.m. In that time she can sometimes entertain as many as 10 clients and earn £50.

The method by which Jean was enticed " on the game " is extremely common and the men who prey on girls often wait at London main-line stations for them.

The usual technique is to pretend that the man's sister has a spare room which the girl can use for a small rent.

Of course, no rent at all is charged and the girl's debts grow as time passes. Her benefactor, who naturally lives in the same house and has been paying her attention, then announces at the right psychological moment that he is in debt, too, and persuades the girl to settle it as in the first case.

If the right kind of help can be given to a girl when she has left home and is " lost " in the big city, she can be saved from drifting into vice.

Valuable work is being done by the London Y.W.C.A. Accommodation and Advisory Service.

Director of the service, Mrs. Rosamund Blackler, told me: " We have greatly expanded the service to cover help with personal problems.

" I estimate that over a year at least 20 per cent. of the girls who come to us are in desperate need of help with some serious personal problem such as pregnancy.

" We have to be extremely understanding and quite unshockable, but the trouble is that so many young girls are so convinced that they can look after themselves when this is not the case."

From *The People*

Life in Britain 30 years from now? Contraceptives in the water and . . .

A TAX ON BABIES

A BOOK is about to explode on Britain that will undoubtedly set off shock waves of anger and indignation.

It is a terrifying book in parts. Only 30 years from now, it suggests, giving birth to a child could be a grave social crime. And it forecasts:

The country will be so overcrowded that the Government might make birth control compulsory and mix contraceptive chemicals in the water supply.

Or family allowances and tax concessions may be stopped to discourage parenthood and there might be a luxury tax on prams, nappies and toys.

This is not the fictional future envisaged by an imaginative novelist. The predictions have been drawn up with clinical precision by Dr John Loraine, a medical researcher.

Dr Loraine, in *Sex and the Population Crisis,** warns that unless drastic action is taken now to curb the soaring birthrate the solutions he lists could become official policy.

" There still remains the possibility that life in the 21st Century and beyond will be tolerable for those destined to inhabit the planet at that time," he says.

Storm

" If (Governments) fail to act now, future generations will inevitably pay the price and the reckoning will assuredly be grim."

Dr Loraine, who is likely to provoke a storm from religious bodies, writes:

" It took the whole of man's existence on this planet to reach the present total of 3,600,000,000 but at the anticipated rate of increase the population will have doubled in as short a time as 30 years.

" This situation is unique in human history and is fraught with peril."

Of Britain he says: " It is obvious that a major element of Government propaganda must be to persuade parents that it is in their own interest and in the national interest to have fewer children."

Children should be taught about birth control in the classroom, Dr Loraine recommends.

" No programme of sexual education in schools would be complete without strong emphasis on the world population crisis and of the clamant need for the limitation of reproductive activities by all the means at present at our disposal.

Traditional

" There can be no question that in the world of the 1970s men and women must swiftly change the traditional attitudes to reproductive processes.

Dr Loraine reviews various suggestions for encouraging smaller families. They include:

Tax benefits for unmarried people, childless couples and parents with small families.

Abolition of family allowances or their withdrawal after an agreed number of children have been born.

Increased taxation for extra children.

Lower maternity benefits for mothers who already have several children.

Avoidance of tax policies that discriminate against working wives.

No subsidised housing on the basis of family size.

But Dr Loraine does emphasise that these policies must contain safeguards for very poor families.

" Apart from such economic changes favouring a reduction in family size, governments could also make it known that they approve of the postponement of marriage," he adds.

Many Church people, particularly Roman Catholics, will find Dr Loraine's conclusions offensive.

But from his home in Edinburgh he said: " I'm not criticising Catholic theology in this book at all.

" The only criticism comes in relation to the Catholic method of birth control which, of course, is well known not to be as reliable as others."

*_Heinemann Medical Books_, 30s.

● That's the controversial view of author Dr John Loraine, whose book appears this week

Now Marcella is having the last laugh

BLONDE Marcella Michelangeli started on her film career because of a joke. This promising young Italian actress was entered in a beauty contest for a laugh by some of her friends. To their surprise, she went through with it—and won.

The result: drama lessons, parts in several plays, TV appearances and then two years ago, the lead in a film. Now, with leading roles in four films, 23-year-old Marcella is well on her way to stardom. She has, so to speak, had the last laugh.

From *Sunday Mirror*

5 Ways to Kill a man

There are many cumbersome ways to kill a man:
you can make him carry a plank of wood
to the top of a hill and nail him to it. To do this
properly you require a crowd of people
wearing sandals, a cock that crows, a cloak
to dissect, a sponge, some vinegar and one
man to hammer the nails home.

Or you can take a length of steel,
shaped and chased in a traditional way,
and attempt to pierce the metal cage he wears.
But for this you need white horses,
English trees, men with bows and arrows,
at least two flags, a prince and a
castle to hold your banquet in.

Dispensing with nobility, you may, if the wind
allows, blow gas at him. But then you need
a mile of mud sliced through with ditches,
not to mention black boots, bomb craters,
more mud, a plague of rats, a dozen songs
and some round hats made of steel.

In an age of aeroplanes, you may fly
miles above your victim and dispose of him by
pressing one small switch. All you then
require is an ocean to separate you, two
systems of government, a nation's scientists,
several factories, a psychopath and
land that no one needs for several years.

These are, as I began, cumbersome ways
to kill a man. Simpler, direct, and much more neat
is to see that he is living somewhere in the middle
of the twentieth century, and leave him there.

Edwin Broc

Sometime During Eternity

Sometime during eternity
                                    some guys show up
and one of them
                    who shows up real late
                                            is a kind of carpenter
        from some square-type place
                            like Galilee
            and he starts wailing
                            and claiming he is hip
            to who made heaven
                            and earth
                                    and that the cat
                who really laid it on us
                            is his Dad

        And moreover
            he adds
                    It's all writ down
                                on some scroll-type parchments
            which some henchmen
                        leave lying around the Dead Sea somewheres
            a long time ago
                        and which you won't even find
    for a coupla thousand years or so
                        or at least for
        nineteen hundred and forty-seven
                                of them
                to be exact
                            and even then
        nobody really believes them
                            or me
                                for that matter
        You're hot
                they tell him

        And they cool him

        They stretch him on the Tree to cool

            And everybody after that
                                    is always making models
                of this Tree
                                with Him hung up
        and always crooning His name
                                and calling Him to come down
                    and sit in
                            on their combo
                as if he is *the* king cat
                            who's got to blow
                or they can't quite make it

            Only he don't come down
                                from His Tree
            Him just hang there
                        on His Tree
                                looking real Petered out
                        and real cool
                                and also
                according to a roundup
                                of late world news
            from the usual unreliable sources
                            real dead

                                            Lawrence Ferlinghetti

By Choi Min Shik

'Brides of Christ'

NUNS are in love with God.

"Yes, really in love," said the girl in the long white habit standing near a piggery in Surrey. She was Irish, very healthy, a bit amused.

"Look, this is sentimental, but you know how a wife thinks about her husband all the time and tries to bake well and look after the house nicely to please him, well we're the same with God. We think about Him all the time and everything we do is for Him. I mean things like cleaning the pigs out are all for God really."

She is one of the Franciscan Missionaries of the Divine Motherhood at Ladywell Convent, Godalming. It is a large Edwardian house, well-proportioned, furnished mainly with huge polished furniture and little Catholic ornaments, full of the sound of quick sturdy footsteps, whisperings and rustling gowns. Intermittent bells break the day and the quiet into a thousand bits. Outside well-kept gardens roll on to farmland and in the distance there are woods.

The nuns are working everywhere – hard. They get up at five most mornings (Sundays and feast days are excepted) spend 2½ hours in chapel before breakfast and then get cracking. There is ploughing to be done, bricklaying, cobbling, printing, farm labouring, as well as all the domestic jobs. They bake their own bread, make jams, sew their own habits and stitch intricate vestments for use in their chapels. The convent has an atmosphere of peace and meditation, but it's deceptive because the nuns' day is a hectic sandwich of hard physical work, prayers, spiritual conferences and recreations.

A sister explaining some of this grinned: "I'm sure you thought we'd be flowing about being delicate and frigid. God's not interested in glamour you know. And it's not as if we're here as refugees from life. We're brides of Christ. God is our outlet."

A senior sister interpreted. "There was this friend of our family's who told my father I must have been crossed in love. That's psychologically daft. Imagine – 80 jilted women living under one roof. Ridiculous.

"I decided when I was about 12. I thought it out very logically. I knew I wanted to love and be loved and I looked about and wondered where I would find someone whom I could really love *always*, and who would really love me – and then I thought God, that's who I'll love, God.

"When you've been in love with God you don't want anybody else. You only want to love Him more and to do more to make Him loved."

The most difficult thing for an outsider to understand is how they know what God's will is. But there is no doubting its strength. A vocation often starts as an irritating compulsion. A woman whose five daughters had gone into the same convent said: "It's the same thing every time. For about a month before they go they are very quiet, a bit depressed. They know they are leaving everything. Yet they surrender with joy – if God wants them they have to go." Several nuns said they had fought the compulsion.

Once inside they become entirely involved and barely notice the fact that they can be visited by parents and friends only at three-month intervals.

Their new orbit has its own complex hierarchy and goals, both spiritual and concrete. This particular congregation was formed in 1935, the first English congregation to specialise in maternity work. It evolved through a much older group which had dwindled to a total membership of six. In 30 years they have attracted 400 sisters and built up 31 bases throughout the world.

The head of the congregation, the Mother General, who is the foundress, displays a bride-like innocence about money matters. "I leave all that to God. He is the man. The woman's job is just to look after the home."

God is helped in several ways. For instance, a group of sisters working in a lay hospital in Singapore lived on absolutely the bare minimum for 10 years and added their pay packets to public donations to build a hospital.

There is a lot of smart thinking about. When they want to do any new type of work they get the best advice and invest in the best training. Sisters have been sent to medical school, building and printing classes. The building team made a large swimming pool and a printing works. The printers produce pamphlets and magazines. The first sister to graduate from medical school came top of her year.

They believe in flexibility of skills, and quite often make drastic changes at the drop of a hat. A sister who was nursing in a leper colony was switched to managing their 90-acre farm. A simple ability to organise got her through the first patch. Now, after eight years, she can hold her own on every technical detail. She is building up a herd of pedigree Friesians with pigs and poultry as sidelines.

The farm doesn't aim to support the convent – one day's yield of eggs wouldn't go round. The sisters eat very well: Mother General agrees with Napoleon that soldiers march on their stomachs. But they eat in silence, and never if they can help it with outsiders.

A cornucopian hospitality is lavished on visitors who stay in the guest house – a small cottage by the main gates. Girls seriously wondering whether to join the congregation stay here for occasional weekends.

A twenty-one-year-old nurse said: "I am seeing what my future home is like." She hoped to move in in six months' time – "God willing". "It's been very difficult telling my parents. They were furious. They said all sorts of things. They didn't mean them. They aren't Roman Catholics you see."

The girl was converted two and a half years ago. "Then after I'd been received into the Church there was this intermittent niggle at my side, but I kept brushing it away. I thought *I* can't be a nun. That's not for *me*. There was no thunderbolt."

She still goes out with boys occasionally – she said there is no reason why she shouldn't. "No, I've never been in love. I hope that if I met someone now I would have the strength to get over it, to still come here. Well, it's only human love isn't it? Oh, I know it's God-given and all that – but it's not the same."

God seems to be a better husband than most men. Mother General said robustly: "Well, look at their faces. They look happy enough, don't they?

"The doors are wide open. Why don't they just go?"

Researched and photographed by Eve Arnold. Written by Pauline Peters. From *The Sunday Times Magazine*.

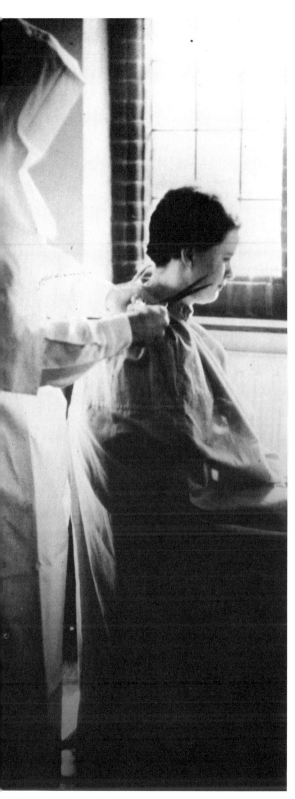

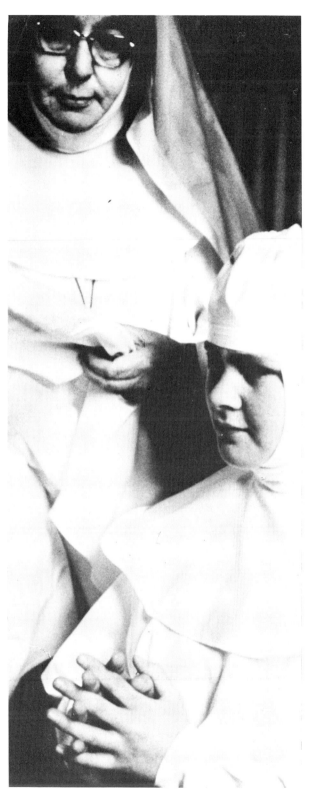

The clothing ceremony at which a nun receives her habit is very similar to a wedding. The sisters call it an 'espousal to Christ'. After the symbolic cutting of a few locks of the 'bride's' hair at the altar, it is later cut very short (left) so that she can wear the tight-fitting headpiece (right).

The postulant emerges from the ceremony as a novice and at a tea party afterwards (top) cuts her 'wedding' cake. The nun's working day is a sandwich of hard physical work, prayers and lessons. As well as cobbling (bottom), they run their own farm, print pamphlets, bake their own bread, lay bricks and deliver babies – the Franciscan Missionaries of the Divine Motherhoo specialise in maternity work.

God?

The Ancient of Days by William Blake

Meeting Human Needs

Jesus did not proclaim the coming of God's kingdom with the demand for dogmatic belief about Himself. His call was not 'believe this and that about me', but to *follow me*. Neither was it any attempt to persuade men to be over-concerned with their own personal holiness. It was a call to let their love go out to their fellow men. It was a call to heal the broken-hearted, to preach deliverance to the captives, to restore sight to the blind and 'to set at liberty them that are bruised.' It was 'To undo the heavy burdens and let the oppressed go free.' Jesus took this as the programme for building the Kingdom of God. It is as we follow Him in working for this Kingdom that, as Albert Schweitzer said, we learn in our own experience who He is. So, too, we reveal to men the loving Saviour and the loving God.

On the day I write this, after early Communion and prayers together, my curate and I went out into our community. There was Holy Communion to be taken to sick, lonely people; there were urgent hospital visits. Between these I spent some hours with three people who had deep-seated personal problems. Then there were more visits until 9 p.m. when I returned to find four teenagers who had been waiting an hour to see me. These youngsters had experienced a sudden dread of death. Between times, four funerals were taken, and the mourners, I hope, helped and comforted.

It is no use going into a district like a whirlwind! It takes years of living in a community to sense its deepest needs. For much of that time one is simply 'sitting beside people in silence', until some contact is made. Then one senses the 'point of need' at which a person or a community must be met by the power of the living Christ. If one tries to do this, there is no such thing as 'success' or 'failure' by any human criteria.

From *The Forgotten People* by Norman S. Power

This old woman is eighty-one and housebound. What she misses most is companionship. Here two young volunteers are providing it.

New Approach Needed

Should you revisit us,
Stay a little longer,
And get to know the place.
Experience hunger,
Madness, disease and war.
You heard about them, true,
The last time you came here;
It's different having them.
And what about a go
At sex, marriage, children?
All good, but bringing some
Risk of remorse and pain
And fear of an odd sort:
A sort one should, again,
Feel, not just hear about,
To be qualified as
A human-race expert.
On local life, we trust
The resident witness,
Not the royal tourist.

People have suffered worse
And more durable wrongs
Than you did on that cross
(I know – you won't get me
Up on one of those things)
Without much prospect of
Ascending good as new
On the third day, without
'I die, but man shall live'
As a nice cheering thought.

So, next time, come off it,
And get some service in,
Jack, long before you start
To lay down the old law:
If you still want to then.
Tell your dad that from me.

Kingsley Amis

Come Down Lord From Your Heaven

They say you've gone to heaven,
But I have heard them tell
That before you went to heaven, Lord,
You also went to hell.
So come down, Lord, from your heaven,
For if you went to hell,
Come down into the clip joint, Lord,
Come down to us as well.

With publicans and sinners
They say you often dined.
They say a girl who was a tart
With you found peace of mind.
So come down, Lord, from your heaven,
For, if you love our kind,
Come down into the strip club, Lord,
Where only love is blind.

Smoke rises in your churches
To praise your holiness.
Smoke rises from our reefers
To cloud our loneliness.
So come down, Lord, from your heaven,
To call, to heal, to bless.
You know that our smoke-rings
Are signals of distress.

The sick they need a doctor
More than the healthy do.
They say you took a dying thief
To Paradise with you.
So come down, Lord, from your heaven,
If what they say is true,
Come down into this den of thieves –
There's thieves have need of you.

They say you were victorious
Over hell and over death.
We know the hell of heroin,
The dying that is meth.
So come down, Lord, from your heaven,
You whom we can't confess . . .
And be the resurrection
Of this, our living death.

Song by Judith Piepe and Stephen Delft.

(Copyright for the World by
Lorna Music Co Ltd)

By John Goldblatt

Try some purple hearts and you'll see a whole new way of life.

A handful of pills can make you feel pretty good. So good you may not want to come back down again.
So a pusher sells you something stronger. And you end up in a dump like this. Going out of
your mind to find cash for new stuff, to get you over the last lot. Is this the new way of life you're looking for?

Issued by National Lifeline, 10 Wyndham Place W1. A charity organisation for drug after-care.

We are Happy...

Ralph Ricketts inserted an advertisement in the papers asking anyone who considered he was happy to write to him. Here are some of the replies he received.

*　　*　　*　　*

You ask to hear from those who count themselves happy. I am one who does, because I believe that the God who created us loves us, and was revealed to us by Jesus Christ.

Whatever happens to us, we know that there is a God who cares. We do not understand necessarily why evil things befall us or those we love or any innocent creature, but if we hold on to Him in faith and love, knowing that not a sparrow falls to the ground 'without your Father', even in this often terrifying world we shall have an abiding happiness that nothing can take away, though for a time it may be dimmed.

You may object that this is old and hackneyed; it is old, but it is always new.

*　　*　　*　　*

I must first say that I am doubtful of the existence of God; and 'after-life', too, I consider anybody's guess. One therefore has merely to concern oneself with one's brief span on this earth. (This may seem too hopeless for you; acceptance of it contents me.) The object therefore must be to make oneself as happy as possible for that period and this I think automatically involves making other people as happy as possible. One can't be truly happy if one is making other people unhappy; to carry it further, one can't be truly happy unless one is actively making other people happy. One can't finish a treatise on happiness without bringing sex into the picture. I am convinced that it has a great bearing on general happiness, though I am far from recommending promiscuity which must always be unsatisfactory. Someone said to me the other day – and I think it is true – 'Sex is only important when it is unsatisfactory.' i.e. it is something which one should have and enjoy and keep in proportion.

*　　*　　*　　*

As I am 40, and have never been unhappy – except for brief periods of acute pain – I offer a few suggestions.

(1) Happiness for man is a happiness of the *mind*. (This is not my idea, but an old Greek philosopher's.) You can't therefore be happy unless your mind is developed – through some sort of study. I suggest you study any of the following:

(a) The Ancient Classics – probably in English.
(b) Selected plays of Shakespeare.
(c) Selected English poets.
(d) A period of History – say the Napoleonic Age, or the Mediaeval Renaissance.

(2) With Atom Bombs in the background, you can't be happy without a belief in the possibility of some *purpose in human life*. To think of life as a meaningless jumble is enough to make anyone miserable. If you cannot accept any belief in a Creator yourself, at least have a look at men who do. Pay a visit to a monastery, say Downside Abbey (Nr. Bath); Buckfast; Prinknash (Gloucester); Ampleforth (York); Mt. St. Bernard (Leicester). Some sort of faith is a basis for all happiness.

(3) Working for others, especially the young, is to me a constant source of happiness. I have been a Housemaster in a boys' school for 10 years, and the joy of training young boys to realise their own abilities, and feeling their gratitude increase as they grow better able to understand what one has done for them, is to me all that I could ask of life.

*　　*　　*　　*

I think happiness, real deep human happiness is to belong to someone, to be loved, to be always surrounded by love; for if you know you are beloved, then you will want to cry when you behold a glorious sunset, a beautiful work of art or things of great beauty which bring a lump to your throat. If you are bereft of love you will not see these things or want to cry about them.

But without God none of these things are possible, for Divine Love is Life, Truth, and all substance. If you know and love God you will find the deep spiritual happiness that most men crave but are unable to find; the need is very great and the longing very deep. I find that unhappy lost humans are usually in need of spiritual comfort.

*　　*　　*　　*

Wearing a white flower turn up at Number 2 Lounge, W—— Court, S.W., between 6 p.m. and 7 p.m. on Thursday, 5th August, and we will make you happy!

From *We Are Happy*, edited by Ralph Ricketts.

...But Most of the World is Hungry

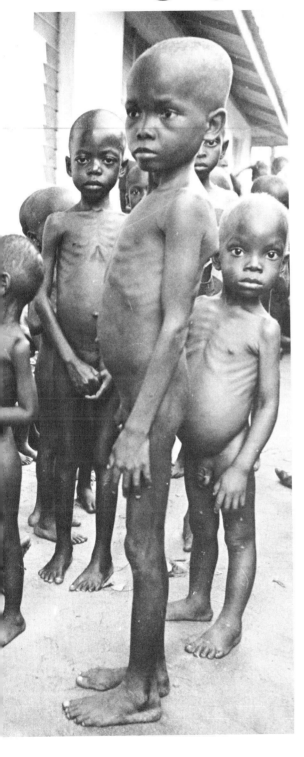

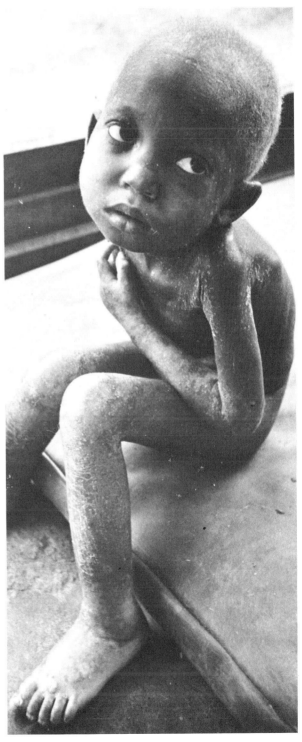

The Young...

...And the Old

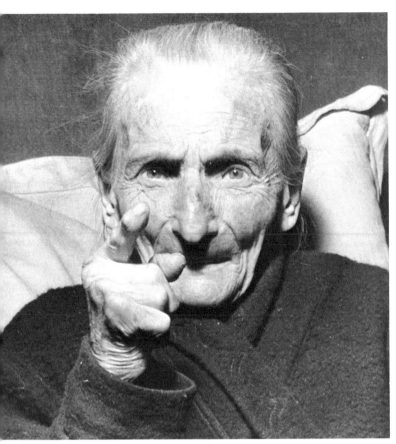

◀ Her hundredth birthday.

Old Comrades. By W. E. Carden.
▼

Resurrection

Is it true that after this life of ours we shall one day be awakened
by a terrifying clamour of trumpets?
Forgive me, God, but I console myself
that the beginning and resurrection of all of us dead
will simply be announced by the crowing of the cock.

After that we'll remain lying down a while . . .
The first to get up
will be Mother . . . We'll hear her
quietly laying the fire,
quietly putting the kettle on the stove
and cosily taking the teapot out of the cupboard.
We'll be home once more.

By Vladimir Holan.
From *New Writing in Czechoslovakia*, translated by George Theiner

By Val Perrin

◀ *The Resurrection, Cookham*
by Stanley Spencer

Invitation

Do you like this book? You are invited to write to the editor and tell him what you think about it. Address your letter to:

The Editor,
'Link Up',
Evans Brothers Ltd.,
Montague House,
Russell Square,
London WC1B 5BX